Connie + Dave —

We're all in
this together !, May
the Lord bless you
and your loved ones.

Sam Anderson

AT THE END OF
YOUR ROPE,
THERE'S HOPE

AT THE END OF YOUR ROPE, THERE'S HOPE

PARENTING TEENS IN CRISIS

Susan Noyes Anderson

Deseret Book Company
Salt Lake City, Utah

Library of Congress Cataloging-in-Publication Data

Anderson, Susan Noyes, 1952–
  At the end of your rope, there's hope : parenting teens in crisis / by Susan Noyes Anderson.
    p. cm.
  Includes index.
  ISBN 1-57345-249-1 (hb)
    1. Parent and teenager. 2. Problem youth. 3. Parenting. 4. Parenting—Religious aspects—Mormon Church. I. Title.
HQ799.15.A55   1997
649'.125—dc21
                              97-36163
                                CIP

Printed in the United States of America   72082

10 9 8 7 6 5 4 3 2 1

Take courage, my friend, though shadows assail.
A new day awaits you, the light will prevail.

To David, Matthew, Karin, Ryan, and Todd—
my eternal family.

CONTENTS

ACKNOWLEDGMENTS

I AM BLESSED with a wonderful family, whose affection, understanding, and good humor nurture my creativity. They are a constant source of joy in my life and being their wife and mother is my favorite calling. Much love and appreciation belong to my husband, David, and my four children, Matthew, Karin, Ryan, and Todd, for their wholehearted support and unqualified respect for this and every project. I disappear into my office for hours at a time when I'm writing, so Dave and those of my children who still live at home deserve high praise for their patience and long-suffering, as well as for their help in the kitchen!

I would also like to thank Nikki Noyes Blake, my sister and trusted friend, for insightful editing; as well as my mother and stepfather, Darlene and Dick Robbins, for their unadulterated enthusiasm. (Everyone should have critics like these two!) My love and gratitude also to Richard Noyes Sr., Nancy Cathey, Jayne Hofhine, and Rich Noyes—for the important roles they have played in my life as valued members of my family of origin.

Special thanks to George Smith for introducing me to Emily Watts, whose thoughtful suggestion prompted me to make anecdotal additions to the original manuscript. My appreciation also extends to Jack Lyon for his involvement and to Richard Peterson for his considerable efforts in facilitating the process. Finally, I wish to acknowledge Karyn Maag-Weigand, who encouraged me to write for publication in the first place.

INTRODUCTION

If

(for parents of teenagers)

If you can keep your head and not lose favor,
When adolescence makes its grand debut;
If you can trust yourself to never waver,
And always keep an optimistic view;
If you can hold your judgment when teens stumble,
Then watch with loving patience as they rise;
And strive to be forgiving—firm, yet humble,
And loyal, even in the face of lies;
If you can always understand the reason,
Yet never give up looking for the rhyme;
And hold your tongue when silence is in season,
Remembering that all things pass, with time;
If you can seek and find the strength within you,
And neither shrink, nor shun, the grueling fight;
If you can move the mountain, or begin to,
And never, in the darkness, lose the light;
If you can lead when children will not follow,
Yet follow, when you must, where they will lead;
And neither lose yourself, nor wind up hollow,
An empty vessel, sacrificed to need;

If you can do all these and never falter,
Nor doubt, nor pause, nor ever give up hope;
Then you are made of stone, just like Gibraltar,
And every other parent is a dope!

I hope Rudyard Kipling will forgive me for borrowing the structure of his original work to illustrate my point. Did you, in reading my fractured version of this famous poem, instantly begin measuring yourself against the ideal behaviors and qualities described? And, by the way, did you come up short? Most likely you were amused and relieved to get a reality check at the end. Not one of us is a perfect parent, and we need that reality check once in a while, especially when we are dealing with teens in crisis.

As the second of five active and rather creative children, I can remember my mother using a time-honored phrase, "I'm just about at the end of my rope!" Generally, this was at the conclusion of a long day, a day we had managed to fill with unprecedented amounts of chaos and confusion. The good news is that she, like other parents, succeeded not only in keeping her equilibrium but in surviving and enjoying our childhood! This not inconsiderable triumph has inspired me to borrow her words for the title of this book, *At the End of Your Rope, There's Hope.*

I do not intend to make light of your very real struggle, for I know from my own experience that parents of errant teens face unique and complex challenges, but it is still possible to maintain equilibrium, survive, and—this is probably a stretch right now—even *enjoy* the teenage years. Does that seem unlikely, even impossible? Is the end of your rope dangerously near? Then take courage and comfort in knowing that you are not alone. Feeling as though the ground has dropped out from underfoot is a sensation shared by many mothers and fathers whose teens are in trouble. Not a few of them, myself included, have known the peril of clinging desperately to our own fraying edges, wondering how much longer we could hang on. Thankfully, we belong to a growing community of parents who are beginning to find safety and security in weaving their broken strands together, creating a network of support for one another. These combined efforts provide a cradle of hope that will keep us all from falling.

The truth we have uncovered is simple but profound: no matter what is happening with our teenagers, all is not lost. Much can be done to sustain and encourage these young people, and many of us who labor as parents have recovered our footing and regained solid ground by applying the information, examples, and suggestions set forth in these chapters. Increased understanding of the issues, combined with specific techniques for intervention, will help you and your teens come off conquerors (see D&C 10:5). Remember, our children were reserved for these difficult times because of their valiance. They had, and have, the right stuff. We parents have the right stuff, too, especially when armed with knowledge and personal revelation.

May the pages of this book lighten your hearts and enlighten your minds with the same sense of hope and inspiration I have felt in writing them.

> . . . And listening, we somehow come to know
> that in the midst of darkness, even then,
> He sends the moon and stars to light our way
> and promises the sun will rise again.

1

IF YOU CAN'T SEE THE FOREST FOR THE TREES, CUT THEM DOWN

AS A WARD Young Women president, I have often been blessed with opportunities to experience the love parents have for their children. I see them attending meetings as families, participating in wholesome activities, laughing and playing together. I am a frequent and delighted observer of spontaneous hugs, wrestling matches, and ticklefests. Sometimes I am lucky enough to catch a glimpse of special teaching moments, in which parents and teens are deep in conversation. I love my calling and especially appreciate what it has taught me about parents and the profound feelings they have for their children. I also love what it has taught me about my own children and the depth of my feeling for them. Most of all, I am grateful for the example other parents have been to me as I struggle to raise my children in an imperfect world.

Knowing I am not alone in this endeavor makes me stronger, especially during times of crisis. Parents need solidarity, and I am eager to join forces with others who are called to this great work of parenting. Some of us may struggle in silence; while some speak freely of our fears and heartaches. In either case, there will be times when mere words are not adequate to express the depth of feeling this stewardship evokes. In these moments, a shared look or gentle touch can bring understanding and comfort, reminding us that we need not struggle alone.

We all love our children, and every one of us is fighting for them. Though we did not seek this battle, it is ours, the unwelcome gift of a fallen brother who would like nothing better than to take our children with him. His entire being is focused on making our young people forget two things: who they are and who they can become. I am convinced that we are here to remind them. That is my belief, but I also believe the key to success will be unity. To that end, and with a spirit of optimism, I offer my love and support— my solidarity, to every one of you. Our methods may be different, but our intent is the same—to ensure the safety and happiness of those whom the Lord has entrusted to our care.

Is there anything on earth more precious than the powerful, visceral relationships we share with our youngsters? How joyful these relationships can be, and how painful. How deeply satisfying they are, yet how terrifying. Indeed, the sky seems to be the limit when it comes to the multitude and diversity of feelings we can experience as adolescence explodes on the scene. It does tiptoe in softly for some, but for many of us it hits like a tornado that whirls down our street and decides it likes the neighborhood. Of course, we like the neighborhood too—the way it *was*. It isn't too surprising, then, that we might try to cope by pretending the twister isn't there, or becoming so used to the push and pull of the winds that we no longer notice them. This chapter is for those of you who find yourselves standing in the eye of a storm that took you by surprise, a storm you did not see coming.

Let's begin with a few questions. Are you concerned about your teen? Do you find yourself wondering where normal adolescent behavior leaves off and trouble begins? Are you uneasy about your child's friends and activities, or lack of friends and activities? If you answer yes, maybe the time has come to suspend the daily routine, find a quiet spot, and set aside a couple of hours to carefully evaluate your teenager.

Most parents will find this evaluation hard to make. Anyone with experience knows that parenting is a difficult job, by nature. Perhaps this is why I have found myself looking to nature for suitable analogies and descriptions. For example, even the best of us, or maybe I should say especially the best of us, feel a few tremors with the mysterious advent of adolescent behavior. When enough of that behavior is undesirable, those tremors can become a full-fledged earthquake, complete with aftershocks. What's worse, we never know when the tsunami's going to hit!

Can anyone be at ease with the ground moving beneath his feet? Even the most stalwart among us are knocked off center when something or someone makes such a dramatic and unexpected shift. Often, we are horrified. Just as often, we remind ourselves that all teenagers, no matter how well-adjusted, go through periods of rebellion and that testing or questioning parents and values is part of growing up. Our internal discussion continues with a review of the dreaded and dreadful X-factor: teenage hormones. Before we are through, we have convinced ourselves, sometimes prematurely, that all is well in Zion.

Of course, in some families with teenagers all *is* well. But in most families, even Latter-day Saint families, one or more teens may need extra help and attention. How can you tell if one of your children qualifies? The first step will be making an honest effort to open yourself up to that possibility. Arrange to spend a day of evaluation compiling a list of all the warning flags you have seen in the past year. Begin with a prayer for clarity, courage, and comfort. Now write down the things that concern you, one by one, without trying to analyze or explain them. Just make the list, going from past to present, leaving nothing out. Here is an example, including specific events as well as general observations:

1. Last Christmas he wouldn't get his hair cut for the family picture.

2. He took down all his sports posters and put up posters of rock groups.

3. He got a referral at school for cutting classes.

4. He quit the debate team.

5. Over the summer, he met some new guys and started hanging out with them.

6. He said his old friends were lame, and they stopped calling.

7. He changed his mind about going to soccer camp.

8. He didn't seem to have much fun on our summer vacation at Lake Powell.

9. When school started he didn't go out for football or basketball.

10. He has stopped carrying his backpack and rarely brings books home.

11. Every Sunday it's harder to get him up for church.

12. When he's home he stays in his room most of the time, playing loud music.

13. A few times he has gone to sleep right after school.

14. He stayed out till 2:00 A.M. last month and didn't even call.

15. We confronted him about his curfew, and he got so mad he punched the wall.

16. He just got the worst report card he's ever had and doesn't seem concerned.

17. He smelled like cigarettes when he got home last night. When I asked him about the cigarettes he yelled at me.

18. I find myself walking on eggshells around him.

19. He talks about getting a tattoo.

20. He just doesn't care about the same things he used to.

How long is your list? Are the things on it one-time incidents, or do you see a pattern developing? If you do see a pattern, allow yourself to look at it clearly, without rationalization or explanation. Now read the list again slowly, experiencing your reaction to each item. Are you uneasy? Anxious? Take a minute to turn your attention to your body. Does it feel tight, queasy? Are you flushed, cold, shaky? It is important to take this valuable time to listen to yourself. You have been called as a parent, and the Lord has blessed you with the mantle of that stewardship. Trust your impressions and instincts, as He has trusted you. Remember that no one on this earth loves your child more than you, and that qualifies you for the work (see D&C 4:5).

Of course, there are pitfalls and potholes along the road to good parenting, and we must be aware of them. Sometimes parents, especially Latter-day Saint parents, are too naive to recognize the gravity of their children's situations. There are families in our midst who have had so much success being in the world but not of the world that they simply cannot imagine the dangers and temptations their children are exposed to at school and in the community. I will tell you about one such family:

> Brother and Sister Martin were a wonderful couple, loved by every member of the ward for their inability to think ill of anyone. Their spirituality was evident to all who saw them, for it shone in their eyes and faces. The innocence and virtue of these good people lifted and inspired others, and their obvious love for their children, all daughters, was beautiful to see.

Interestingly, these girls were full of vinegar and could be quite mischievous, yet their parents were models of patience and forbearance. They were consistent and loving in their correction, enforcing good boundaries firmly, but gently. As the children grew, they became solid citizens at school and at church. They were hard workers, willing to donate service and often seen in leadership positions. The Martins' good parenting skills were paying off for the whole family.

Unfortunately, one of their daughters, an accomplished athlete, injured herself rather severely in a diving accident. Though she was not paralyzed, she suffered trauma to her back and jaw that sidelined her from sports for many months. In addition, she was forced to take steroids to combat inflammation, and her appearance was marred by swelling and weight gain. As her former self-confidence plummeted, she began to behave differently. Some of her friends, uncomfortable with her changed looks and personality, began to avoid her. Feeling lonely and betrayed, this young girl reached out for the wrong friends, friends who offered easy acceptance and a chance to "tune out" her problems and struggles. Before long, she began using alcohol.

Her parents, intelligent and caring as always, knew she was in trouble. Sadly, they did not know all the reasons why. It seemed logical to assume that her problems were purely emotional, and while emotions were indeed at the root of the girl's drinking, the drinking itself went unrecognized. She was loved and supported by her family in every way that occurred to them, yet she continued to fall more deeply into what eventually became addiction. Fortunately, concerned about their daughter's emotional health, the Martins asked their bishop to recommend a Latter-day Saint therapist for help with their daughter's depression. In the course of that treatment, her alcohol use was discovered and addressed in an excellent outpatient program.

It had not occurred to the parents that their child could be drinking. In fact, this was so far from their frame of reference that they never even suspected it. To their credit, they knew there was a problem and did not cease to look for help until it was identified and resolved. When they were told by the therapist that substance abuse was suspected, this courageous couple prayed for confirmation and were finally able to receive a witness that their daughter, a good and lovable girl, was in trouble with alcohol. When they asked her why she had not been completely honest with them, she answered that she "loved them too much to disappoint them that way." Clearly, the children of good parents are not immune to the world and its dangers.

The Martins made some mistakes, but they also did a lot of things right. None of us is going to be a perfect parent, but we can all ask ourselves this question: If my child is in trouble, am I willing to know? Sometimes being willing means letting go of fear or guilt. Other times, it means educating yourself as to the real problems and possibilities. Nearly always, it means taking a leap of faith and exercising a belief in God's ability to lead and sustain those who seek Him. One thing is certain—if we will open our minds and hearts to listen, the Spirit will tell us the truth about our teenagers. And truth is a very good place to start.

How can we be open to receiving this kind of personal revelation about our children? When a child who has always been trustworthy gets off track, we may be diverted from the truth our spirit is sensing by the untruths our child is telling. Never a shrinking violet, when I became concerned that my teenager was making some bad decisions, I began to confront him openly. He was usually ready with explanations for his behavior that minimized or even seemed to explain it away. It would be easy to tell you that his past record of honesty was responsible for my failure to see clearly what was happening, and to some extent that would be true. It would also be true to say that I, though to a lesser degree than Brother and Sister Martin, was naive. There was, however, something else at play as well. I didn't want to believe that my son could be in trouble, and I used his past record of honesty to protect myself from knowing the truth. As a result, I believed him far longer than was good for either of us. In other words, I couldn't see the forest for the trees.

With that in mind, take a serious look at your forest. If overgrown trees of denial are all you can see, don't be afraid to cut them down. If that's more than you can do right now, maybe you could just prune them a little. It may take some time and effort, as it certainly did for me, but that time and effort will be well spent. I wanted my child on the right path, but I couldn't help him get there until I began to recognize and identify the path he was traveling. Fortunately, our Father in Heaven is aware of each and every path His children take. He not only sees the forest clearly, He directed our Elder Brother in its creation. Surely He will direct us too, not only in finding out where our teens really are, but in creating the most nurturing environment for their growth and eternal progression.

HELPS AND HINTS

TEN STEPS FOR CUTTING THROUGH DENIAL

1. Pray for courage, inspiration, and an open mind.
2. Educate yourself.
3. Try to observe objectively.
4. Get input from family members.
5. Listen to feedback from other parents who know your child.
6. Meet with your bishop or youth leaders to share fears and ask questions.
7. Interview school teachers and leaders.
8. Sit down and converse frankly with your child in an atmosphere of love and concern.
9. Arrange evaluation by a licensed professional, if needed.
10. Always prepare for the worst; always hope for the best.

Red Flags for Teens at Risk

1. Hangs out with a different group of friends.
2. Studies less; "never" has homework.
3. Talks to parents less.
4. Ignores or challenges curfew.
5. Acts sullen, disrespectful, angry.
6. Acts moody or apathetic—has higher highs and lower lows.
7. Doesn't want to do things with the family.
8. Doesn't call or hear from old friends anymore.
9. Doesn't bring new friends home.
10. Grades are slipping; losing interest in once-valued hobbies or activities.
11. Taste in clothes is changing.
12. Prefers extreme hair style.
13. Listens to heavy metal or other extreme music; obsesses over rock groups.
14. Spends a lot of time alone in room.
15. Yells at parents; openly challenges authority.
16. Sleeps more, especially during the day.
17. Shows interest in piercing, tattoos.
18. Gets referrals or is suspended for cutting class.
19. Smells like cigarettes; denies smoking.
20. Doesn't want to attend church; jokes about or won't discuss the Word of Wisdom.

Please note that this list is not all-inclusive, and your child may not demonstrate all symptoms or may show other signs not listed.

Make it your business to notice and evaluate changes in your teen's behavior. Any one of these red flags can be cause for concern and should not be dismissed lightly.

That's Parenthood

Somewhere behind the angle of your face
resides the soft cheek of a child I knew,
well hidden from an undiscerning view;
a casualty, perhaps, of time and space
or maybe just gone missing, with a trace.
Is there no kinder path to your debut?
This separation game of peekaboo,
unyielding, puts me firmly in my place . . .
then takes me out again to walk the wire,
(each foot as tentative as unshed tears)
afraid of falling in the line of fire,
precariously perched upon my fears.
That's Parenthood. I wish I could retire
and meet on neutral ground in seven years.

2

HOW TO AVOID GOING DOWN WITH YOUR TEEN'S SHIP

A CLEAR VIEW of the path a troubled teen is traveling can feel like an icy plunge into a sea of confusion. Remember Alice in Wonderland, struggling to stay afloat in her ocean of newly shed tears? How will we successfully navigate our own waters of despair? Can we avoid going down with what may seem like a rapidly sinking ship?

There is nothing more agonizing than watching young people we love make choices that jeopardize their eternal salvation. Few parents can remain calm and unruffled when a child is in danger. Awareness that a teen is being lured into worldly traps and snares strikes fear into any mother's or father's heart, and it is crucial to recognize and deal with this powerful emotion. Sometimes it is easier for us to identify other feelings: anger, sorrow, and hurt, for instance, but it is important to understand how fear forms the underlying basis for these.

Example 1: We may be *angry* with our child because he is making bad choices. Why do we care whether he is making bad choices? Because we are *afraid* for him, or for ourselves, or both.

Example 2: We are *sorrowful* because we are grieving our child's bad choices. Why are we *grieving* those bad choices? Because we *fear* that the child will be lost to us and may lose his eternal salvation in the process.

Example 3: We are *hurt* because we feel betrayed by our child who has made bad choices, and perhaps, *hurt* because we feel judged by others. Why do we feel betrayed by the child's choices and judged by others? Because we are *afraid* our child may not love or respect us and *afraid* that we may lose the love and respect of others.

Most fear comes from the knowledge, often subconscious, that outcome cannot be absolutely controlled. Several years ago, I eagerly accepted my first position as a marriage, family, and child counseling intern. Listening closely to the people who came to me as clients, I observed two things that may be applicable here: (1) Where there is a strong agenda and limited control, fear is a natural by-product. (2) The best way to deal with and move through this fear is to face it head-on. Of course, we cannot face it if we are not aware of it.

Let me share the experience of a couple I will call the Dunlaps:

> The Dunlaps were an admirable family in many ways. The righteous parents set a good example, and ward members respected their commitment to teaching gospel principles. Family home evening was held regularly, with fun activities every week. People often noticed what a good time this particular family had together.

Eventually, their youngest child began to show the telltale signs of teenage rebellion. At first, there was nothing dramatic—a change in musical taste, an interest in rock shirts and posters, and a few C's on his report card. He was still doing his chores, attending school regularly, and playing ball, but there were new friends who seemed uncomfortable around the family. Also, though he continued to be close to his brothers and sisters, he attended church meetings less willingly than before and seemed particularly resistant to Tuesday night youth activities.

Being conscientious parents, the Dunlaps were concerned about the changes in their son's behavior. They had successfully avoided these behaviors in their older children, and while neither wanted to talk about his or her fears, both were quite worried. A couple of attempts to bring the subject up for discussion had only seemed to make matters worse. Mom and Dad had plenty of ideas about what they needed to do, but couldn't seem to reach an agreement about how to do it. Finally, not wanting to create unnecessary distress for the other by making a mountain out of a molehill, each made a private decision to work on correcting these relatively minor problems before they became major ones. Surely the efforts of a committed and determined parent would get the boy back on track.

He had always been a good child, so the mother began by wondering what she might be doing wrong. She knew it was important to remain objective, but the more she thought about it, the worse she felt. Perhaps it was all her fault. Maybe her son needed more attention than the other children. Had she been too hard on him? Expected too much of him? Been overly controlling? Before long, Mom was making up for her real and imagined inadequacies by giving up almost all of her personal needs and interests to indulge his. Nothing was too much to ask, and there was nothing she wouldn't give him if he would only listen to the things she needed to say. Sometimes he would not listen, and she would cry because she had failed him so miserably. Other times her fear for him would be like a pain in her stomach. Their relationship deteriorated as he tired of her emotional lectures but periodically pretended to agree with her in order to get the material things and privileges he wanted.

Brother Dunlap, on the other hand, decided the boy was spoiled rotten. Maybe he had enjoyed his youngest a little too much, been too much of a buddy and not enough of a father. The older children would never have dreamed of such behavior, and this son must be called strictly to account for every imperfection, large or small. He promised himself that he would do whatever was needed to make his child obey. As patriarch of the family, he accepted his responsibility to raise righteous sons, and no amount of vigilance could be spared. Of course, as the boy grew more rebellious, his behavior became more undesirable. Now Brother Dunlap clamped down even further, forced into a stance that was unfamiliar to him. Trying desperately to rescue his son, he became tougher and more critical. The entire feeling in the family was changed, and Brother Dunlap grew increasingly angry about the situation. He felt as if the boy's behavior compelled him to do and say things that made him uncomfortable. Often, after a particularly severe argument, he would feel bad about himself. How could he be trying so hard and failing so miserably? Why did he feel guilty all the time? He even began to wonder if he was a worthy priesthood holder.

As for the son, he was convinced that his father didn't

like him. "Not that it matters much," he'd say. "I guess we were never that close anyway." Asked about his mother, he would complain that she was just the opposite. She cared about him too much, and most of the time he wished she would just back off.

Unfortunately, the situation escalated. This confused young man, who was well-loved but didn't know it, was clearly in trouble. There were problems at school; there were problems at home. There were even problems with the law. One look at him and you knew he had lost his way, and members of the ward did look at him—with great concern. Sensing their friends' interest, Brother and Sister Dunlap became convinced that others viewed their family as a failure. They feared people were criticizing them. Sister Dunlap blamed herself, while Brother Dunlap blamed his son. Both were bitterly unhappy and resented the strain on their thirty-year marriage. When their son was eventually caught selling hallucinogens, the parent-child relationship had deteriorated to the point where the court ordered family counseling. Now, even the marriage was in trouble. Mother, father, and son were thoroughly depressed, though they acted it out in different ways.

Here was a family in crisis, but there was still much room for hope. Perhaps the court-mandated therapy could provide a forum for everyone to address problems openly and sort things out. Together, they would make sense of things. They would tell the truth, share their feelings, and come to an understanding. At long last they would come up with a healthy and united plan of action. This was the hope, but it was never fully realized. Yes, the Dunlaps did attend therapy, but the real issues were not addressed. Fear ran too deep and had become so firmly entrenched that they couldn't seem to move past it. As a family, their self-esteem was low, and their self-doubt was overwhelming. Perhaps they had hidden the truth from themselves so long that they didn't know how to find it. Maybe they had suffered to such an extent they didn't know how to stop.

Still, some of the surface tensions were smoothed out a little. Family members treated each other more politely, and the young man did agree to a period of sobriety. Meanwhile, his parents tried their best to forgive him and each other, though their success in doing so was limited. Regrettably, he was unable to forgive them completely either. He just didn't know them well enough and knew even less of the fears that had driven all of them.

Fear kept the family from reaching a true resolution, and that same fear sent the errant son back to his drug use. Now that he has reached adulthood, the parental stance has become one of denial. They hope he is doing fine, and he tries to look as if he is. The rest of the family seems to be getting along fairly well, and the Dunlaps are clearly trying to move forward and make the best of things, but I can't help thinking that important pieces of them went down with their son's ship. What's more, these good people were unable to throw him the life preserver he so desperately needed.

Fear is indeed a force to be reckoned with, but that force can be greatly diminished by meeting it squarely. As Latter-day Saint parents, we know that "perfect love casteth out fear," (1 John 4:18) and that "God hath not given us the spirit of fear; but of power, and of love, and of a sound mind" (2 Timothy 1:7). Naturally, we want to exercise our faith in that direction, and sometimes, like the Dunlaps, we skip a step in that process. That step is acknowledging that our fear exists. It is true that God does not wish us to be fearful, but he also knows that even the best of us will be. If good, faithful people did not experience fear, the Lord would not deal with that subject so frequently in the scriptures. Being omniscient, He knows and understands our weakness. Understanding our own weakness enables us to develop the strength we need to survive the rough seas of parenting.

Indeed, how can fear be overcome if we are unable to recognize it?

Remember when Jesus told Peter that, before the cock crowed, he would deny Him thrice? (see Matthew 26:34). The Savior knew that Peter would be afraid, and He was sharing that information, as well as the outcome, with Peter. As it happened, Peter was not sufficiently humble to listen, but instead assured the Lord that he would never deny Him, under any circumstances, even if it meant his death (see Matthew 26:35). Perhaps if Peter had been willing to acknowledge his vulnerability—his *fear*—he could have prepared himself better. He might have devised a reasonable plan that would have allowed him to cope with his fear constructively. Instead, he permitted that feeling to dictate his actions and felt awful about it afterwards.

What if the Dunlaps had admitted their fear, reminded themselves that they were still good people, and made a plan of action that would have created a safe and honest arena for their son? Would he have navigated his difficult adolescence, as well as its accompanying problems, more easily?

As parents in the Church, we have a strong agenda. In fact, it is an uncompromising one—we want eternal life for ourselves and our children. We have everything to do with our own success and much to do with encouraging the success of our children, yet any real control of their outcome is limited. No wonder we become frightened! All we can control is ourselves and our parenting, and even that is not easily accomplished. Of course, we can humble ourselves, recognize our weakness, and, with the Lord's help, turn it into strength (see Ether 12:27), but only our children can make the choices that will lead them back to our Father in Heaven. They have their agency, and watching them abuse it can be terrifying.

Sometimes this terror, particularly when unacknowledged, turns even the most well-meaning parents into tyrants, so bent on controlling and dominating that we neglect to love and teach. This type of reaction sets us up for failure, because we are taking on a task beyond our reach. By giving in to fear and the need to control, we compromise our ability to help our children. Instead of working in their behalf, we begin working in our own behalf, allowing our personal insecurities to drive us. Our focus goes from understanding what *they* need to demanding what *we* need, or think we need. This is how the power struggle, a dynamic not limited to the Dunlap family, is born. Brother Dunlap got so caught up in controlling his son's behavior that he lost sight of his original goal—teaching his son to use his agency wisely. In the heat of every rebellious adolescent moment, it is easy to forget the divine and universal gift of agency.

Overlooking this gift is a sure-fire way to jump on board a teen's sinking ship. Not only do we jump on board, but we try to take over the helm, forgetting that the Lord is the captain, because now we are confusing our own safety and well-being with our child's. Propelled by fear, we lose all objectivity as we place ourselves in the same deep water he is battling. Often, we become angry with him for making us look bad. We begin to wonder if others are judging us. It seems clear that "everyone" believes we are bad parents, and pretty soon we agree. Guilt takes over. Surely we must be the worst of parents for our child to make these kinds of mistakes. It's all our fault; we've ruined him. We are failures. As our self-esteem erodes, we render ourselves less and less able to help our teenager, sinking into a downward spiral of guilt, grief, feelings of inadequacy, and self-pity. Too many parents have navigated these waters.

What's wrong with this picture? Everything. Our children's behavior is about them, not us. Resolve, for your sake and your child's, to keep the focus where it belongs. You are you, and he is he. You may not be a perfect parent, but you have done your best, or at least the best you knew at the time. Would you like to do better? Get more information and pray about how to proceed. Any parent stands to benefit from greater education and spiritual awareness. If you decide you want or need to make a few adjustments, that's okay, more than okay, as long as you do it in the right spirit. In other words, don't *guilt* yourself into better parenting, *love* yourself into better parenting.

Do you really believe others are judging you by your child's behavior? If so, work harder on not judging yourself. That privilege is reserved for the Lord and should be left to Him. Repent wherever you need to, then forgive yourself. Remember that other parents, good parents, have felt the pain of seeing their children make bad choices. Cain slew Abel; Laman and Lemuel were rarely obedient. And what of Lucifer? Our Heavenly Parents are perfected beings, but their son still had his agency. The parent who gets caught up in blaming himself is the parent who can't be there for his child.

On the other hand, parents who work through their

own issues openly, honestly, and prayerfully can leave that downward spiral behind and become solid allies for their teen. By addressing our emotions constructively, we can avoid getting stuck in the quagmire of grief, guilt, and gall the Dunlaps experienced. All parents dealing with troubled children will struggle through powerful feelings. What we do about those feelings is of the utmost importance in redirecting that child's life.

There are no guarantees, but if we can separate from our children enough to parent not just firmly, but fairly and wisely, the chances for their success will be multiplied. What's more, we will have the comfort of knowing we have done our best.

By the way, doing our best doesn't mean that we do a perfect job, that our teenagers are trouble-free, or that every crisis has a happy outcome. The Dunlaps didn't do everything wrong, and even if it had been possible for them to do everything right, their son would still be the determining factor in his own destiny. Doing our best simply means that when faced with difficulties we make every effort to behave judiciously, address issues constructively, accept help where needed, and in general, avail ourselves of all the opportunities at our disposal. Perhaps even more important, we accept responsibility for preparing and maintaining ourselves adequately to support our children when they do falter. If we feel ineffective—and sometimes we will—we gird up our loins, repent as needed, and try again.

Being rather intimately acquainted with the girding and repenting process myself, I know how much energy it requires. Take time to fill yourself up and replenish your strength daily, for good self-care is a key ingredient of effective parenting. You are engaged in an exhausting endeavor, one that frequently demands that you put yourself and your emotions aside to nurture a troubled teen. Be sure to balance your self-sacrifice with some fun, relaxation, and spiritual pursuits. Dance, meditate, study the scriptures—swing on swings at the park if it makes you feel lighter—but do more than one thing a day that makes you feel good and recharges your battery. Make a point of actively building your self-esteem, which may be shaky. Reach out to other mothers and fathers, offering them the same love and understanding you are seeking. Remind yourself that you are a loving and responsive parent. Have a good cry if you need to. Make two fists and shadowbox some of that anger away. Rent some Laurel and Hardy movies and giggle all night. Spend time with good friends, eat well, increase your spirituality, get enough sleep, and exercise regularly. Just do it. Take that time for yourself because you deserve it. If that seems too selfish, remember that the only way you can be a supportive parent is by remaining well, staying strong, and keeping your perspective.

In fact, it is especially helpful to keep the entire struggle in perspective—eternal perspective. Remember who your teen is—a spirit brother or sister who made the same courageous choice you made. This valiant spirit chose to come to earth, receive a body, and learn to govern it. He believed in himself and chose wisely then; maybe you can believe in him and his ability to choose wisely now. If you exercise your faith in this way, perhaps your belief in him will help him remember his belief in himself. This is a meaningful way to live the gospel, and it sets a loving example for your child. You don't need to go down with your child's ship. Keep yourself afloat, then you can throw him a life preserver.

HELPS AND HINTS

HOW AM I, REALLY?

(a self-test to identify Empty Cup Syndrome)

	Always	Sometimes	Never
1. I wake up in the morning feeling refreshed.	A	S	N
2. I get 6 to 8 hours of sleep.	A	S	N
3. I eat tasty, nourishing meals.	A	S	N
4. I get regular medical and dental exams.	A	S	N
5. I do exercise that I enjoy.	A	S	N
6. I make time for hobbies and activities I enjoy.	A	S	N
7. I spend time during the week enjoying nature.	A	S	N
8. I laugh.	A	S	N
9. I spend time with good friends.	A	S	N
10. I am comfortable calling friends when I need to talk.	A	S	N
11. I plan adequate quiet time for myself.	A	S	N
12. I go on special dates and getaways with my spouse.	A	S	N
13. I ask for help when I need it.	A	S	N
14. I can say no when I am overbooked.	A	S	N
15. I am able to forgive my own mistakes.	A	S	N
16. I feel good about myself.	A	S	N
17. I receive enough physical affection.	A	S	N

18. I feel loved.	A	S	N
19. I read my scriptures.	A	S	N
20. I pray regularly.	A	S	N

If you have fewer than ten A's or more than five N's, your cup needs a good filling!

A Promise for Eternity

I think somehow
that long ago
in the eternities,
I was a special friend to you
and you a friend to me.

We shared a bond,
an understanding
that was quick and sure.
I wonder if we knew that it
would deepen and endure.

The tie between us
had to be
a very special kind—
for even in this earthly life
our paths have intertwined.

We were sisters,
bound by a love
so meaningful and rare,
that we must have had an inkling
of the destiny we'd share.

And once prepared
to leave the heavenly
sphere we'd always known,
surely we joined hands and vowed
to help each other home.

Now that we find ourselves
mother and daughter
on this earth,
please don't forget the vow we made
and its eternal worth.

For though I know
that in this life
the burden rests with me,
the promise we two sisters made
was for eternity.

3

STEWARDSHIP, NOT OWNERSHIP

THE MORE I SEE and understand the powerful effect parenting has on children's lives, the more awesome that responsibility feels. Apparently, even small things we do during the various stages of our child's development can influence his adult well-being. Taking that into consideration along with our imperfections, this parenting assignment we share seems a bit overwhelming. That being the case, what exactly is our stewardship as parents? The best answer is found in examining the role of a perfect parent, our Father in Heaven. How does He parent us, and what might we take from His example?

Let's begin by looking at the amount of control the Lord exercises in our lives. "Of every tree of the garden thou mayest freely eat" were His words to Adam and Eve in support of their agency. Yet He told them not to eat of the tree of the knowledge of good and evil and warned that there would be dire consequences if they did, "for in the day that thou eatest thereof thou shalt surely die" (Genesis 2:16–17). As we all know, they exercised their freedom to choose, ate of the tree, and became subject to death; but even then all was not lost. The Father had a plan—a plan of salvation—guaranteeing immortality and offering eternal life, conditional upon the choices they would make. As parents, we must have a plan for our children as well, a plan that both allows them their agency and sets forth rules and consequences if they abuse that agency.

> Sister Mack, a delightful woman who had recently been widowed, was frequently visited by her next-door neighbor, a young mother of three boys. These boys loved to spend time in Sister Mack's living room, which was brimming with trinkets and treasures. Unfortunately, their visits were somewhat less enjoyable for Sister Mack herself, who watched in horror as the boys' mother ran from place to place, intervening to avert one disaster after another. Conversation was next to impossible.

The frazzled young mother was continually apologizing to Sister Mack, explaining that she didn't know why her boys wouldn't obey her instructions not to touch. All the parenting books said to be consistent, and that's just what she was doing. In fact, she kept after those boys from the second they walked in the door to the second they left. "What more can I do?" she asked one day, feeling helpless and hopeless. "I just can't control their behavior."

"Leave 'em home," answered Sister Mack. "Let 'em learn to control their own."

Self-mastery, of course, is a process, but how does it relate to our stewardship? I think Sister Mack understood a principle we sometimes forget. Nephi teaches that "ye are free to act for yourselves—to choose the way of everlasting death or the way of eternal life" (2 Nephi 10:23).

Therein lies the unsettling truth: Just as we are free to act for ourselves, our children are free to act for themselves. We are not commissioned as parents to deny children this freedom, nor can we exercise it in their behalf. The Lord will not allow it. What He does allow are consequences: some natural, some God-given, some parental. We who are called to be mothers and fathers determine what those parental consequences will be, as well as how and when they get exercised. Of course, success is most likely when our consequences complement the natural and God-given ones we are supplementing. Rules and limits should be in keeping with higher laws as well, all with an eye toward helping our children achieve self-mastery.

Why is self-mastery so important? Let's take a minute to look at the Lord's declaration to Joseph Smith: "For your good I gave unto you a commandment" (D&C 61:13). We were given commandments to live by and promised eternal life if we would choose to obey them faithfully. "I, the Lord, am bound when ye do what I say; but when ye do not what I say, ye have no promise" (D&C 82:10). This scripture speaks volumes to parents about the exercise of constancy, obedience, choice, and consequences. Mothers and fathers, too, are bound—bound to love and nurture our children, bound to establish a reliable structure of rules and expectations for them, and bound to allow them to experience full accountability for their choices. We can make no blanket promises to them, for to do so would exceed the limits of our authority. Rewards are predicated upon obedience, and every one of our teens has the right and duty to choose for himself the way he will go.

Does our children's agency neutralize us as parents? Absolutely not. Our position is a powerful one; we act as servant, exemplar, tutor, and guide. We teach, but they must learn. We speak, but they must hear. We establish rules and consequences based on true principles, but it is they who must ultimately be held accountable. We cannot protect them from themselves, and we cannot force-feed them either. Every good thing we offer them as parents can be received only by choice, their choice. That is why it is so important to wrap the gifts of truth and knowledge we give them in unconditional love, so they will choose to open them, see their beauty, and eventually possess them. Let me illustrate with this example:

> One talented and capable woman, greatly admired for her position as mayor of a certain community, had a young daughter. As a growing girl, this daughter continually asked her mother to spend more time at home, and promises were made and broken by a mother who found it difficult to extricate herself from civic responsibilities. Eventually, the daughter came to resent the hours her mother put into community service, as well as her part-time job as a realtor. The mother would like to have been home more often, but tried instead to compensate as much as possible with what she called quality time, carefully engineered to give her daughter solid leadership, effective guidance, and sound moral principles.

When this particular girl entered high school, she began to cut classes. Her truancy was a source of great embarrassment to her mother, who had often stressed the importance of encouraging parents to be proactive in enforcing school attendance. When the school notified this chagrined parent, she reacted by letting her daughter know, in no uncertain terms, that for every day she missed school she would miss a full weekend of activity. For a while, this acted as a deterrent, but it wasn't long until the girl became truant again and found herself grounded for months ahead. Feeling angry and trapped, the girl defiantly refused to go to school at all. Her concerned mother responded by taking a month off work to personally escort her daughter to each and every class. Naturally, leaving her job for this amount of time was an imposition and the mother bitterly resented it, blaming her daughter vocally for their growing financial concerns.

Needless to say, the situation deteriorated. Mother and child could not seem to come to an understanding, and though the daughter stopped short of dropping out of school entirely, she began to wear clothes and makeup that almost screamed her anger and rebellion. Of course, this was a source of sadness, rage, and embarrassment to the mother, who reacted accordingly. Over the next year or two, this troubled relationship escalated into a battle of incredible proportions, until the daughter was eventually arrested for shoplifting and the mother was forced into practicing tough love, a last resort she was not comfortable with and which was not entirely successful.

The moral of this story? Limits must indeed be set, but first, make sure that needs are met.

The mother in this vignette loved her daughter, but did not seem to appreciate the importance of being emotionally and physically available enough of the time to make that love felt. Many women work to support a family, but this mom saturated her free time with extracurricular activities, to the detriment of her only child. Limits and discipline cannot exist in a vacuum. Boundaries are important for teenagers, but they will rarely be recognized or respected in the absence of openly expressed and internalized love and affection.

The stewardship we hold as parents is a sacred gift

from our Heavenly Father. It affords us the opportunity to practice the art of loving unconditionally, placing the welfare of others above our own. We experience joy and sorrow as we watch and learn from the spirit brothers and sisters who are our children. We gain a deeper understanding of the fallacies of Satan's plan every time we attempt to exercise unrighteous dominion, driven by fear into misguided efforts to force our children's obedience and safety. We can only do what we can do, just as Jesus Christ did all that He could do for us. In the end, even our most loving sacrifices and valuable offerings can be received by our children only in the exercise of their God-given agency. These children do not belong to us; they belong to themselves. What a blessing it will be, in our lives and theirs, if they choose to belong to their Savior as well.

Choice is the key word, but remember, that does not change the character of our stewardship. We must be careful not to confuse our children's free choice with a free ride for their parents. The Lord charges us with great responsibility in raising our children, as He made clear in this revelation given to Joseph Smith in Ohio: "Inasmuch as parents have children in Zion, or in any of her stakes which are organized, that teach them not to understand the doctrine of repentance, faith in Christ the Son of the living God, and of baptism and the gift of the Holy Ghost by the laying on of the hands, when eight years old, the sin be upon the heads of the parents. . . . And their children shall be baptized for the remission of their sins when eight years old, and receive the laying on of the hands. And they shall also teach their children to pray, and to walk uprightly before the Lord" (D&C 68:25, 27–28). Our stewardship is to teach.

What else does the Lord expect of us? He has

commanded us to "bring up [our] children in light and truth" (D&C 93:40). This requires creating an environment that encourages righteous living and provides a solid structure for growth and progression. We will not succeed unless we establish the kind of loving relationship with our children that nurtures obedience and trust.

Parenthood is a divine calling and a difficult one. Apparently, we are required to give our all. Nobel Peace Prize winner, Dag Hammarskjold, once said: "You have not done enough. You have never done enough; so long as it is still possible that you have something of value to contribute" (*Markings* [1964, 1969], 158). We have much that is of value to contribute as parents, not the least of which is respect for our children's agency. President Joseph F. Smith said, "This is not the way God intended in the beginning, to deal with his children—by force. . . . You can't force your boys, nor your girls into heaven. . . . You can only correct your children by love, in kindness, by love unfeigned, by persuasion, and reason" (*Gospel Doctrine* [1939], 316–17). We teach correct principles and establish necessary limits, but it is they who must learn to respect and embrace them. We can love, encourage, apply consequences, and pray with all our might, but in the final analysis it is our children who must come to know for themselves the freedom that comes from living within righteous boundaries.

> Controlling the winds may be out of our reach,
> but adjusting our sails is not. We cannot adjust
> our teenage children's sails, but maybe, if we catch
> enough wind and get up enough speed, they will like
> what they see and decide to adjust their own.

HELPS AND HINTS

ACTION VERBS FOR PARENTING YOUR CHILDREN BY THE SCRIPTURES

Be happy in	Maintain
Bless	Make known to
Bring up	Minister to
Chasten	Prepare
Command	Provide for
Defend	Provoke not
Despise not	Remember
Exhort	Suffer them
Give good gifts to	Teach
Hear	Train
Let them know	Weep for
Love	Withhold not correction

Your Own Identity

You want to make decisions for yourself,
to find out who you are and what you'll be.
Sometimes you push the boundaries as you search
for something called your "own identity."
I watch in fear, in love, in pain, in trust,
wishing that I could do this work for you.
I cannot, for in growing you must choose;
but choosing does not alter what is true.
For truth is truth, before this world and now.
Freedom is lost in immorality.
The Savior's course is one eternal round . . .
a loving sphere, a sacred boundary.
And when you choose to live within His sphere,
beyond the reach of every deadly snare,
you'll recognize yourself as God's own child
and find your place beside Him, as His heir.

4

AN OUNCE OF PREVENTION

NOW THAT WE'VE talked about the incredible stewardship we possess, let's put on the whole armor of parenthood by reviewing some information and education about teenagers in general. Before we embark on what seems like a peace-keeping mission in a foreign land (and what could be more *foreign* than the world of our teenagers?), we'd better make sure we know the terrain . . . as well as the natives! Can you imagine the United Nations making a move without adequate reconnaissance and intelligence-gathering? Why should *united parents* be any less informed?

Let's start with the basics. Most moms and dads agree that teens, as a group, tend to be strong-willed. We are painfully aware that there are times when the need for self-determination takes the form of defiance. As mentioned in Chapter 1, some defiance is a normal part of the separation process. Given that fact, it might be useful to ask ourselves what our particular definition of a defiant teen is. What does that phrase mean to us?

Some mothers and fathers label a teen defiant if he or she is not a clone of themselves. These parents would do well to remember that our teenage children are not us and do not exist to satisfy our egos. They are made in the image of a loving Father, who created them from preexisting intelligences and celebrates their differences. Like their parents, young people have a right to their own views of the world, their own personalities, and their own agency. If we do not respect their need for self-expression and independence, it should come as no surprise when they begin to fight us for it.

I once heard a story about a young man whose family, for generations, had maintained a proud tradition: every male child became a doctor. To his father's dismay, and in spite of a real fondness for medicine that he managed to ignore in his rush for independence, this particular young man reacted to what he considered excessive pressure by deciding to shun the family profession. Adding insult to injury, he selected a career in musical theater. Naturally, his father was appalled, a very satisfying state of affairs for the newly acclaimed thespian. Though his talent was only passable, he ended up remaining in show business for years before he finally realized that medicine had been his real love all along, obscured by parental interference and expectation.

Do we label our teens defiant if they are unlike us? Hopefully not. Teens who have different ideas from ours or like different things are not, by definition, defiant. They may *become* defiant if they are not allowed to be themselves. Teens, and all of us, need the freedom to be individuals. They are not clones, nor should they be. A better definition of a defiant teen is "one who rejects parental influence and guidelines to engage in self-destructive behavior, making choices that jeopardize his physical safety, emotional well-being, and spiritual growth." This kind of teen is not acting in his own best interest.

Who decides what's in a teen's best interest? Ideally, this is a shared job. Until the teen is an adult, our stewardship is to teach and protect, which gives us a certain authority in determining what is best for him. With such authority comes a sacred responsibility to make sure our own interests don't take precedence over his. "What man is there of you, whom if his son ask bread, will he give him a stone? Or if he ask a fish, will he give him a serpent?" (Matthew 7:9–10). We need to give good gifts to our children. Our efforts in behalf of young people should be about their safety and well-being, not ours. Teenagers have an uncanny knack for knowing when a parent is acting out of self-interest. They will lose respect for us if we tell them something is for their good when it is really for our own.

> My daughter has a school friend whose parents have often made this mistake. They are extremely overprotective and have been quite restrictive with her activities. Over the years, this well-liked girl has missed most of the sleep-overs, many birthday parties, and even her boyfriend's senior prom at a nearby high school. Though her parents' reasons often sounded thoughtful and protective, it didn't take long for this sheltered daughter to decide that they were looking out for their own interests, not hers. The last straw was when they offered to pay her five hundred dollars to miss her senior prom! This, of course, was so she could avoid all the "wild parties" and "drinking." Assuring them she had no interest in attending wild parties and

that drinking was strictly prohibited, she declined what she called their bribe and attended the prom as planned. She did not attend the after-prom party, which, by the way, was held at my home—not exactly a den of iniquity!

There are two painful realities to this true story. One is that my daughter's friend has lost respect for her parents because of their efforts to manipulate her. The other is that she has been so overprotected that she now lacks self-confidence. All the other girls in this group are going away to college, but this girl, an excellent student, has opted to stay home and attend junior college because she is afraid to spread her wings and fly.

What truly lies within our sphere of influence as parents? What belongs to our teens? Where do we share responsibility? Parents always have input, but the more respect we earn by not stepping on agency, the more teens will allow us to affect their behavior and decisions. Let's look at a few areas of choice that are important to our young people:

Area of Choice	Parental Domain	Teen Domain
personality	nurture, influence, mold	form, adjust, finalize
interests	expose, encourage	cultivate, adopt
hobbies	offer opportunities, support	choose, enjoy
school, knowledge	set and enforce rules, encourage, inform	scck, accept, learn
beliefs, values	teach, encourage, model, share testimony	receive, internalize

Area of Choice	Parental Domain	Teen Domain
church	set example, require attendance (if possible)	be converted, endure
friends, social life	influence, make rules, set curfews	select, befriend, obey
self-presentation	set limits (choose battles carefully!)	express self
behavior, activities	set rules, enforce consequences	opt to control behavior
thoughts, ideas	teach, model, try to influence	think, decide, become
abilities	support, encourage, provide opportunity	develop, maximize
talents	identify, support	recognize, magnify
health	provide medical care, teach hygiene	make personal choices
safety	teach	make judgments
hygiene	model	put into practice
sense of responsibility	set expectations, guidelines, enforce	internalize, act upon
accountability	hold them accountable	hold selves accountable
work and vocation	teach them, make suggestions	work, choose vocations
role in family	set expectations	meet expectations
curfew and other family rules	set and enforce limits	respect, obey, cooperate

Clearly, teenagers have a wealth of opportunity to exercise free agency. What tools can we use to ensure that our input is valued and our authority respected? Fairness and consistency, respect for them, respect for ourselves, unconditional love, good two-way communication, and solid relationship skills are of the utmost importance. How do we achieve these things? It helps to have started from birth, but it is never too late to begin. Teenagers are smart. If we are selling them short, they will notice and return the favor.

Listed below are some additional issues to consider in parenting our adolescent children. Some of this will be review, but bear with me, because the best defense in parenting really is a good offense. Or to put it another way, being proactive now can save a lot of trouble later.

1. Separation. In the beginning, our children are totally dependent upon us. Separation is necessary for each child to become an independent adult. Sometimes this is an easier process than other times. If we have allowed our children some freedom and decision-making responsibility as they've grown, separation will be easier. If we have been overly controlling, our children are probably somewhat enmeshed with us and will find the process more difficult. These children may use defiance in an attempt to break away. We can help avoid this defiance by respecting agency and individuality, allowing children to make more of their own decisions as they become able, and giving them freedom in whatever areas we can so they learn to take responsibility.

When young people do make a mistake and get off track, it is never productive to fixate on parental guilt, agony, or pain. If an error has been made in our parenting, the best course is to recognize it, correct it, and move forward, grateful that repentance is available and aware that perfect parents do not exist. Every time we turn undesirable things our teens do, think, or say into self-defeating statements about our own worthiness, we compromise our emotional health. Where changes need to be made, we should greet such changes with a spirit of optimism, empowering ourselves to think clearly and act courageously.

As the shocked mother of a teen who had suddenly veered off track and was eagerly challenging every limit and belief, one of my first reactions was wondering where I could have gone wrong. I knew a parent should not expect to do everything correctly, but I couldn't help feeling I had made some major error, or my son would not have been so confused. Surely I had done something out of the ordinary (and I don't mean *exceptional!*) for him to get so lost. As time went by, these concerns began to weigh on me, and I felt the burden of his struggle in my own life. Many times I went to pick him up at school and found that he wasn't even there. Then I noticed other mothers looking at me sympathetically and felt somehow diminished by their concern. It was as if I had become a second-class citizen in my own eyes because my son chose not to be obedient. I saw myself as the object of everyone's pity and worried that if my son didn't respect me, perhaps no one else would either.

Fortunately, I had enough counseling experience to question those negative thoughts and made a point of challenging the false beliefs that threatened to erode my self-confidence. I reminded myself of all the good parenting I had done, then took an honest look at mistakes along the way. I observed that many parents made the same mistakes I had, or similar ones, and still had obedient children. Though I had not been perfect, I had done my best and was not personally responsible for my son's poor choices.

Finally, I concluded that the biggest parenting error I could ever make would be allowing myself to become a victim of my child's confusion. The last thing he needed was a mother who was as lost and confused as he was.

I have since learned from my son that he did respect me; he just wasn't showing it at the time. I also learned, first-hand, that my friends and associates had not been pitying me. They had felt empathy for my suffering and respect for my efforts to stand by my son. The point is simple: If we feel good about ourselves before our teenagers get into trouble, we can continue to feel good about ourselves during and afterward. If we do not feel good about ourselves, there is no better time than now to begin. We need to feel good about ourselves if we are going to help our children.

The tendency to experience a teen's problems and disappointments as if they were our own is a common trap for well-meaning parents. We love our children most selflessly when we are able to *separate*. Psychologists illustrate this idea with a story about a young man who tells his mother he has diabetes. By the next day, *she* is taking insulin. Before long, the codependent woman is sicker than he is and in no condition to help him whatsoever. Even worse, all the comfort and attention he needed has suddenly been shifted to his mom, who winds up in the hospital being treated for insulin shock. We cannot fix our children's problems, nor can we heal them by swallowing every bitter pill that comes their way.

Enmeshed parents are as vulnerable as their distressed children. Adult perspective can be lost by identifying too closely with a child, making it difficult or impossible to provide effective, nurturing support. We need to be the safe place for our teenagers. If their errors or sorrows bring us down, who will they turn to? Remember, we want to be rooted in solid ground so we can be there to throw them those life preservers. It is important to love and care and support and guide, but as one older and wiser child of God to another, not as enmeshed parents.

2. Limits. It is a good idea to set firm limits and enforce them with steady hands and a cool head. We are most effective when we maintain neutrality, establishing limits and then allowing those limits to have a life of their own, as if they existed independently.

Once reasonable limits are in place, consequences for violation can be administered in a friendly, even sympathetic way. There are few parents who enjoy the role of Enforcer. Why not point this out to our teens? We can share their disappointment when they earn a negative consequence, but let them know we love them enough to do our job, even when it hurts. Remind them that we are expected to help them learn accountability and responsibility and that negative consequences are part of that process—and part of life. We can, of course, suggest that positive consequences are also available! Making discipline fair, being consistent, and using natural consequences where possible will go a long way towards improving relations with our adolescent children.

3. Authority. We would do well to explain parenting to our teenagers. As mothers and fathers, we have jobs to do. These jobs are stewardships, divine callings from God. We should help our children understand that while we respect their agency, our function is to set limits and try to influence them for good. Reminding teens that we will be held accountable by the Lord if we have not fulfilled our responsibilities (see D&C 68:25) allows them to see unwelcome parental involvement in a different light. It

may be useful to tell them that a day is coming when the veil will be taken away and that they will hold us accountable too, if we have let them down. What could be more powerful than letting our young people know we are not willing to let them down, that we will have done all we can do and said all we can say to guide them, no matter how difficult it is or how uncomfortable they make it for us? What a perfect moment to share the reason we are willing to do all of this—because we love them so deeply. They may still dislike our parenting at times, but at least they will have a better understanding of the process and know that we have their best interests at heart. Of course, this goes back to making sure that we do have their best interests at heart and not our own agendas.

4. Recognizing their agency by loving unconditionally. Certainly the most important thing we parents can do for our children is to let them know they will be loved no matter what they do and then work at making that happen. It is not enough to simply tell them we love them, though this is a good beginning. We need to show our love in a way that makes it real to them. This is the backbone of the whole parenting experience, isn't it?

HELPS AND HINTS

FIVE TOP ANSWERS TO TEEN QUESTIONNAIRE, PART I

(50 teens responding)

Q: What do your parents do that really hurts you?

1. My parents don't listen to me.
2. My parents criticize me when I tell them my thoughts.

3. My parents make negative comments, spank me, or yell.
4. My parents underestimate me and treat me like a baby.
5. My parents get mad at me in front of friends.

Q: What do you wish your parents understood?

1. I wish they understood me and how I feel.
2. I wish they understood my friends.
3. I wish they understood that I am almost an adult and can make some decisions.
4. I wish they understood how messed up things are at school (drugs, etc.).
5. I wish they understood my perspective, not thirty years ago, but now.

These are important answers to our survey and will be helpful in promoting parent/teen understanding.

In a much lighter vein, here are a few more requests your teenager might like to make of you . . .

Rise and Shine (Not!)

Don't wake me up.
Don't pound my door.
I need more sleep.
I need much more.
Much more than you.
Much more than he.
Much more than this
whole family.
Have some respect!
I stay up late.
I watch TV.

I meditate.
I need my rest,
believe you me.
Ignoring you
takes energy!

5

A POUND OF CURE

BEFORE WE DIVE into the mechanics of making a plan, let's go over a few personal survival tips and strategies that can be real lifesavers in parenting any teen:

1. Pick your battles, realizing there are some things you can't control, yet never giving up as a parent. Great strength comes in making a plan and sticking to it, loving the child throughout. It isn't always easy to show love for a child who is engaging in negative behavior, but it can be done.

2. Keep the goal in mind. If your "righteous" anger is damaging the relationship with your child, remember that you probably represent the Church to him. How he feels about you is often how he will feel about the Church. So go ahead and reprove betimes, but don't forget to show forth the increase of love afterwards (see D&C 121:43).

3. Don't be a wimp about making rules. Kids need them, as we all do, but make your rules reasonable. Don't be so restrictive your child must rebel or suffocate. Remember that teenage rebellion doesn't mean they hate

you or are trying to destroy you, though they may be trying to embarrass you. For the most part, they are just doing what they need to do—part of the growth process—and you will make rebellion less necessary by helping them separate and encouraging independence.

4. Have fun with your teens. Be a friend. Build up goodwill so you have some to spare. Log in fun times to balance the ones that may not be so fun, such as when you're having to hold the line on hard issues. Show that you really like them.

5. Use humor with teens. Most enjoy it, but be careful not to make fun of them. Make fun of yourself; they love that!

6. Sometimes letters are better than lectures. Many teens say it is easier for them to read a letter with parental input than to listen to that parent's voice, especially if the material is that kind of "uplifting" information that teens tire of all too quickly. Also, the letter helps keep you from repeating yourself in an effort to sell your points or drive them home. Note: When you are speaking, make your point and then move on. Don't belabor it. Once you've been heard, rubbing it in will only put your child on the defensive.

7. Avoid making negative remarks about friends. This will almost always work against you. Speak in generalities, or ask which friends seem to bring out the best in them, or the worst. Let them know up front that they don't have to answer these questions, just think about them. This is a good device to use in many areas.

If you are concerned about a particular friendship, don't attack the friend. Your child needs to take responsibility for his part of the dynamic. Say something like, "It seems to me that the two of you show better judgment when you're alone than when you're together." You can then move into a more general discussion about how some friends bring out the best qualities in each other and some do not, making way for the topic of whether it makes better sense to choose relationships that are uplifting. Maybe your teen wants to try a limited experiment to see if a particular relationship can be made more positive. Be flexible. You could set up a time limit and monitor the situation carefully, agreeing ahead of time that if there are no results, that will mean it's best to move on. If specific observations are to be made about particular friends, it is wise to let your teen be the one to make them, but in order for this to happen, you must first have created an environment in which the teen does not feel defensive.

8. Get to know your teen's friends, and make your house a comfortable, inviting place for them. Even if you aren't too thrilled with the friends, it's better to know them. Sometimes you can influence a friend when you can't influence your child; then the *friend* can influence your child!

9. Don't be emotionally reactive or they won't tell you anything. Try to keep your cool and be objective, caring, and firm. Again—separate, separate, separate.

10. Don't be pressured into hasty decisions. Tell your teen you need a day to think something over, or a week. Also, make sure you and your spouse present a united front. On big decisions, let your teen know you must consult with the other parent first. Don't let your child play one of you against the other.

11. Begin at a young age to do things as a family, and let your teen develop a sense of community, family ties, and responsibility. Even the most recalcitrant teen will go along with an activity if he is trained in the "as a family"

mentality. If you haven't established this, it's never too late to start.

12. Be trustworthy. Teens can spot a hypocrite a mile off. If you are not being straight with them, they won't be with you. Respect them and be worthy of their respect. Don't give them ammunition to use against you.

13. Make your praise specific. Not, "You're a great poet," but, "I love that line about green hair the color of Sprite cans." Sweeping compliments are often dismissed by teenagers and can make them feel the pressure of unrealistic expectations. When you respond specifically to something concrete they have already done, they can really take it in.

14. When something goes wrong for your teen, try validating his feelings. Not, "Oh well, no big deal, it doesn't really matter in the scheme of things," but, "That really hurt you. You were so disappointed." Don't always try to tidy things up for your child. Being heard and understood helps a teen move through feelings more quickly, developing his own process of resolution rather than depending upon yours.

15. Express your anger when you are angry at your teen, but do not insult. Never attack your teen's personality or character. For example, when you see dirty workout clothes on the floor, don't say, "What are you, a slob? You are always so messy and inconsiderate!" but rather, "When I see dirty workout clothes on the floor I feel angry. Dirty workout clothes do not belong on the carpet. They belong in the hamper!" No one has been injured here, but you've gotten your message across. Remember to describe what you see, what you feel, and what needs to be done. Don't attack the person. By the way, remember that saying "I feel like you're a creep" is

not describing your feelings. "I feel angry" is about your feelings. The rest is name-calling.

16. If you do mess up and overreact or insult, apologize and explain your feelings. For example, "What you did was wrong, but so was my reaction. I was angry, and I'm sorry I didn't handle that better." Respect them even when they are not respecting you. This is important modeling. Don't go down to their level, expect them to rise to yours. If you deal squarely with them, there is far more likelihood that they will deal squarely with you.

17. Let your teen know you are concerned for him. He may feel you are controlling, even when you are parenting wisely. Help him see you as concerned. For example, "I'm concerned that you _____," or "I think _____ is dangerous behavior."

18. Don't make a young person's behavior be about you. Never, "Oh, you're hurting me so much! You're going to be the end of me," but "It's hard to watch you hurting yourself this way." Teens will like your concern more if they feel it's for them and not yourself. Other ways of expressing your concern include: "You deserve better," and "You need to take better care of yourself."

19. Never resort to emotional blackmail. Using a child's love for you as a weapon will only make him more angry and rebellious. He needs to know you are there for him no matter what, but he also needs honest feedback about his behavior. Don't be afraid to hold your teen accountable. He can know absolutely that you love him but dislike something he's doing. Separate the two. Work at it. It is crucial, especially if the behavior has seriously deteriorated. Conditional love hampers development and maturation and produces conditional emotional health and well-being.

20. Believe in your children, and don't forget to share that belief with them often. Having someone believe in you helps when you don't quite believe in yourself, as is the case with most teens. These are uncertain years. Even if they are messing up seriously, believe in their ability to do better. Work at it. Pray about it. Remind yourself they made the choice to come here and get a body, which proves they had gumption and goodness. Trust that, and let them know you trust that. Pray, ask for personal revelation in their behalf, and share that personal revelation with them.

21. Encourage them to get a patriarchal blessing at age fifteen or sixteen, maybe even fourteen if they are mature enough. Having their blessings relatively early in life can help teens navigate the world more safely. Patriarchal blessings give teens a sense of direction and help reinforce worthiness, as well as reasons for staying worthy.

22. Find the right balance of friend and parent. Too much friend isn't good, because the parenting suffers. Too much parent isn't good, because there isn't enough friendly footing to operate from. You can be a good parent and a good friend. When your teen is testing the limits and you're enforcing them, that's the ultimate "parent" moment, but even during that time you can be a friend.

23. Make consequences as logical as possible. If teens drive irresponsibly, they should lose car privileges, not phone privileges. If a curfew violation occurs, make curfew one hour earlier for a week. If homework is not getting done because of video games, restrict *them*, not baseball. Try to make your restrictions selective and specific. Teens need a solid consequence they can feel, but they also need fun and enjoyment in their lives. If you take everything away, they have nothing to fill their cups.

Young people who are running on empty will have fewer resources to use in producing good behavior. Tell them you are enforcing the consequence not because you want to pay them back, but because you want to make it uncomfortable for them so they will learn to be responsible. If they are missing the dance, empathize. Let them know you hate that they're missing the dance. Validate that "it stinks." Consequences often do, but they happen all the same.

24. Contracts are very popular and can work well. Negotiate them together, in as uncharged an atmosphere as possible. Sometimes an impartial third party can be helpful. Set out consequences for violation of the contract ahead of time, before a violation occurs.

25. Avoid power struggles by allowing your teen responsibility for himself whenever possible. If he balks at having his physical exam for football on the appointed day, don't use up energy and goodwill forcing him. Let him know that you have done your part by making the original appointment, and that if he chooses not to go, he will need to arrange for his own exam before the season begins. If he fails to make that happen, step back and allow him to take the consequences. This requires active self-restraint, but resisting the urge to bail him out on the small stuff will pay off. It's amazing what a little life experience can teach.

26. Family council meetings and personal interviews are great tools. Start at an early age if you can, but remember, it is never too late. Let them help determine rules and talk about consequences.

27. Do not allow teenagers to manipulate you. Work on your own self-esteem and empower yourself to be a good parent. Don't allow your child to put you on a guilt

trip. Remember that no one is the perfect parent. Remind yourself of all the good you've done, and if something isn't working, look at it honestly and prayerfully, with a willingness to make changes. Keep the lines of communication open with your child. Set laws and rules together, then enforce them neutrally. Talk to other parents. Form parental support groups. Never give up.

There's a lot you can do, isn't there? Of course, sometimes it will seem like none of this is working. When you are most afraid for your teen, pray for strength, remind yourself to have faith in his divine nature, and then trust him to make it, with Heavenly Father's help and yours.

HELPS AND HINTS

FIVE TOP ANSWERS TO TEEN QUESTIONNAIRE, PART II

(50 teens responding)

Q: What do your wish your parents would do to make things better?

1. I wish my parents would trust and understand me.
2. I wish my parents would listen more.
3. I wish my parents would control their tempers better and not yell at each other or us.
4. I wish my parents would let me make my own decisions more often and be more fair.
5. When they are wrong, I wish my parents would admit it; I always have to say I am wrong.

Q: What do your parents do that really helps you?

1. My parents listen to me when I need to talk to them about problems and other things.

2. My parents love and support me and spend time with me.
3. My parents trust me. They let me have some freedom, but they also keep me in line.
4. My parents encourage me and tell me when I do something right.
5. My parents set a good example and show me what is right.

Just for a Change

Just for a change I'd like to make
a change this Mother's Day—
I'd like to do the things that all
those mothering books say.
I'd like to give up yelling and
perfect the old "I" statement.
Not "Turn that racket down!" . . .
but "I'm in need of noise abatement."
Not "Talk back once more and you're toast!"
but—"I demand respect."
Not "Brush your teeth, or die!" . . .
"I fear your hygiene is suspect."
I'd like to be the kind of mom
who gets the kids to clean
(and they all end up having fun,
and no one thinks you're mean)!
I'd like to be the kind who gets
the dinner on the table,
and never has to set it, 'cause
her children are so able. . . .
And willing, oh, I'd like to be
the kind that makes them willing—
I'd write a how-to book, and

would I ever make a killing!
I'd sort of like to be the type
who's frugal as can be,
and manages her time so well
she's always home by three.
The kind whose kids are never spoiled
because they love to work,
who think a kid who asks his mom
for money is a jerk.
I'd really like to be that kind—
and, oh, just one more thing . . .
I'd like to be the kind who's never
freaked by anything.
The kind who always keeps her cool,
no matter what goes down.
The kind who can control her kids
with one look, or one frown.
(Or two looks or two frowns, or even
one big burst of words!)
I'd like to be the kind who looks
real hip, but not absurd.
In short, I'd like to be a mom
who's good as good can be.
The only problem is, how would
my children know it's me?

6

MAKING A PLAN

A PLAN IS A wonderful thing, and a first-class plan is the best gift we can give ourselves when a child is in trouble. My husband and I were bemused, baffled, and bewildered until we finally came up with ours. Not that it cured us, exactly, but it sure took away some of the pain! It didn't cure our son either—he had to do that himself—but at least we had the comfort of a good protocol to follow. Being at the end of our collective ropes, we were looking for all the structure and security we could get. Having a plan was like putting our feet on firm ground for the first time in months.

Does that sound pretty good? If so, it's time to roll up your sleeves and get busy. Start out with a heartfelt prayer for guidance and direction. An inspired, righteous plan brings comfort in its execution, even when the immediate results are disappointing. What's more, following a well-conceived blueprint guarantees fairness and consistency and ensures that important goals are not obstructed. When we get angry or discouraged (and we will), our teen is protected from resulting errors in judgment, because all the material decisions have already been made. Feelings of hopelessness are overcome (and parental sanity saved) as we learn to measure success by how faithfully we are administering the plan and not by our child's behavior. Celebrating every effort we make in supporting teens as constructively as possible boosts our confidence and reduces fear. There is no better medicine for the ailing teen or parent than a good, solid plan.

An excellent way to begin is by educating ourselves. We need to reach out and get help—at church, in the community, from our extended families, through books and other reading materials, from service organizations, or in consultation with a licensed professional. There are many resources available, and we should take full advantage of them. We cannot make a plan worthy of our teen if we are not informed, and we cannot give a child good information if we do not have it.

One thing that can hold us back is embarrassment. Often, parents of troubled teens will go to great lengths to hide their situation from others. We are much better served by facing these problems squarely and dealing with them openly. People who are left unaware of our struggles cannot be expected to help us or our children. Of course, details should be withheld from all but trusted friends, but there is much to gain in telling our stories to a few carefully chosen allies. Support is a wonderful thing, and all of us need it, particularly in the midst of crisis.

Whether we are married or single parents, the next step is to meet with our parenting partner and actively communicate so we can support one another. Suppose the Dunlaps (Chapter 2) had made a point of sitting down together and hammering out a plan? This may or may not have made a critical difference for their child, but it would surely have made a life-changing difference for them. They would have been partners—sharing feelings, concerns, and strategies in an effort to redirect their son. Together, they could have used the mantle of their parenthood to call down blessings and inspiration that are available to all of us. Instead, they struck out on their own, missing the chance to experience the strength and stability which comes from laboring in unison, sharing and bearing the burdens. They failed to follow the admonition of Paul, "Wherefore comfort yourselves together, and edify one another, even as also ye do" (1 Thessalonians 5:11).

Sometimes this kind of collaboration between parents is easier said than done, but even those whose marriages have ended in divorce will need to find ways of working together as a team in order to succeed. Resisting the urge to blame will be of particular importance. Sharing feelings, observations, complications, and possible ramifications is also essential to this effort. Mothers and fathers also need to review and appreciate each other's parenting style before deciding how to proceed.

When my husband and I began to make a plan for our son, we were amazed at how many differences we had to resolve. Though we had been married for many years, the stress of worrying about our child was bringing out behaviors and opinions we had never seen in each other. He felt that I talked too much when dealing with our son; I felt that he talked too little. He felt that I didn't give our son enough space; I felt that he gave him too much and then some. Under previous conditions, we had developed a combined parenting style that worked pretty well for us. However, this crisis situation forced us to regroup and set some new ground rules. We ended up fashioning an agreeable compromise that allowed each of us to utilize our strengths and play down our weaknesses. We discovered whose style worked best at what time and parented accordingly.

As we parents exert ourselves in behalf of wayward children, we must be particularly sensitive in attempting to understand one another as thoroughly as possible. Analysis and brainstorming are premature until parents are unified.

After doing everything we can to express, discuss, and respect individual feelings and issues, we are ready to begin an in-depth analysis of our teen's situation. All pertinent data should be considered, including the specific personality and level of functioning demonstrated by the child in question. We also need to consider our own personalities, how those personalities interact with our adolescent's, what we might be willing to change, and what we are absolutely not willing to change. It is important to be as flexible as possible, while still respecting our own needs and limits. What are we willing to live with? What does our child require? How far can we push our boundaries? Is there any room for compromise?

Good questions to ask ourselves are: How did we get to this juncture? What, if anything, have we done to contribute to our child's difficulties? What is his own contribution? How is he being negatively influenced by his environment, at school or at home? Is there anything we can do to change that environment for the better? How is his behavior affecting the family? What can we do to minimize negative impact? Where do his areas of weakness and strength lie? How can we best use our knowledge of these to conceive a plan that will support and encourage him? Can we handle conflict constructively? What will we do to defuse hostility and foster cooperation?

As we ask ourselves these questions, some of us begin to wonder if we have squandered too much authority and goodwill fighting skirmishes. Others conclude that they have failed to respect reasonable differences, stifling their teenager or pushing him to be what he is not. Not a few parents are chagrined to realize that no adjustment in their parenting has ever been made to accommodate a growing adolescent. Of course, we are all faced with unique circumstances and must continue to exercise positive leadership, but if we look hard enough we may find creative ways to resolve conflict less painfully while still being true to ourselves.

With our problem-solving process in full swing, solutions begin to materialize. Maybe having a clean room every day isn't quite as important as we thought, so long as the room is ready for deep cleaning on Saturdays. Perhaps curfew can be extended in special circumstances, providing a timely call is made requesting permission. Do these issues seem minor to you? Are you in a place with your teenager where the stakes have gone sky high? Remember that the same principles of compromise hold true with serious infractions. Is your child habitually truant, maybe even suspended from school? It could be that a young person who contracts to attend school reliably, complete and turn in all homework assignments, and be responsible for doing after-school chores for a period of time might eventually instill enough confidence in his parents that they would consider negotiating a driver's license, or paying car insurance, or reversing a punitive curfew.

Our main focus should be keeping the limits realistic

and reasonable, the consequences natural or enforceable. Positive and negative consequences should be equally utilized. Maintaining parental dialogue until we are of one mind and heart will be an essential component in presenting a united front to our teen. This union is especially important if he has been engaging in substance abuse, or otherwise exercising poor judgment. As we proceed, it is critical to carefully evaluate each teenager with particular regard to his state of mind, the quality of our relationship with him, and his willingness to comply. If willingness is a problem, strategies to promote compliance should also be discussed.

Sometimes willingness is only part of the problem. We need to make sure that the plan we design is tailored to fit not only the teen's needs, but his state of worthiness. Remember the law of Moses? It was given to the Israelites because it was what they required at the time, a lesser law intended to teach them obedience while laying the foundation for the observance and understanding of a higher law that would eventually be reinstated. It was a set of rules they could handle, altered because of their state of transgression, allowing little room for personal interpretation. In His wisdom, the Lord devised a law that was appropriate to their situation. Its demands challenged them, but not to a degree that made obedience impossible. The law offered them a chance "to bridle their passions, to overcome the lusts of the flesh, to triumph over carnal things, and to advance to the place where the Spirit of the Lord could have full flow in their hearts" (Bruce R. McConkie, *Mormon Doctrine*, 2d ed. [1966], 435). It prepared them for things to come, for the day when they would be ready to live the higher law.

"And now I say unto you that it was expedient that

there should be a law given to the children of Israel, yea, even a very strict law; for they were a stiffnecked people, quick to do iniquity, and slow to remember the Lord their God" (Mosiah 13:29). Does that sound like any teenagers you know?

"Therefore there was a law given them, yea, a law of performances and of ordinances, a law which they were to observe strictly from day to day, to keep them in remembrance of God and their duty towards Him. But behold, I say unto you, that all these things were types of things to come" (Mosiah 13:30–31). Clearly, a foundation for future understanding was being laid.

"And now, did they understand the law? I say unto you, Nay, they did not all understand the law; and this because of the hardness of their hearts" (Mosiah 13:32).

Did the people of Israel understand the law? No, but they did obey it (or the *letter* of it) and not just because they had been commanded to do so, but because its demands lay within their reach. It made sense to them. As they obeyed, their hearts and spirits were softened. Paul, in an epistle to the Saints at Galatia, explained: "Wherefore the law was our schoolmaster *to bring us* unto Christ" (Galatians 3:24). Our teenage law should be formulated with that same end in mind. Line upon line, precept upon precept, we can bring our wayward teens back to the source of light and truth. We can help them learn obedience by making sure our plans are appropriate and suitable, asking as much of our teens as possible without exceeding the current limits of their capacity.

Indeed, it might be necessary to establish a pattern of compliance with some basic, lower laws before invoking the higher ones, a formula which makes many parents uneasy. Everyone prefers a rapid resolution, but returning to the straight and narrow path can be a painstaking, step-by-step process. Though Alma changed in the space of two days and two nights, most mighty changes take time, and it is the love, planning, and patience we put forth that will most likely enlarge the hearts of our children.

The Psalmist referred to this long-term process of obedience when he wrote, "I will run the way of thy commandments, when thou shalt enlarge my heart. Teach me, O Lord, the way of thy statutes; and I shall keep it *unto* the end. Give me understanding, and I shall keep thy law; yea, I shall observe it with *my* whole heart" (Psalm 119:32–34).

When our preparations, both practical and spiritual, are complete, we should find a quiet time to sit down with our child on neutral ground, firmly stating our belief that he is in trouble. Being direct is crucial. At this point, he may become defensive, and we will need to communicate our concerns clearly and calmly, with as much detail and specificity as possible. Showing our love and goodwill is vital to establishing a working relationship with our teen. Remembering to separate the behavior from the child will make it easier for him to hear us, reassuring him that our support and affection are not lost.

Now it is time to formulate the final plan. Don't forget to utilize the outline "Making a Plan—a Twelve-Step Program and Sample Contract," located in the Helps and Hints section at the end of this chapter. For a fully detailed model of the Twelve-Step Program in action, see "Letter to a Parent," also at the end of this chapter. This letter chronicles a real-life experience and provides many examples of creative rules and consequences and how to implement them.

Of course, your teen's input must be heard and

considered—an integral part of setting up and negotiating a contract. The main thing to remember is that every rule and consequence should be tailored to fit the unique needs of each family. Once agreed upon, these can be spelled out clearly, preferably in writing, to avoid confusion, deception, or default. It is in everyone's best interest to establish a workable plan, firm up the details, and stick with the program. Good luck!

HELPS AND HINTS

MAKING A PLAN—A TWELVE-STEP PROGRAM AND SAMPLE CONTRACT

1. Prayerfully identify areas of concern.
2. Gather information and educate yourself.
3. Reach out (and up) for help and support.
4. Unite as parents; form an alliance.
5. Consider and discuss all pertinent information about your teen.
6. Analyze your parenting style and how it affects your teen.
7. Ask yourself, each other, and trusted friends the hard questions.
8. Experiment with viewing the situation from different points of view.
9. Brainstorm hypothetical solutions, letting go of rigidity and opening to new ideas.
10. Compile a tentative list of limits and consequences—considering your teen's needs and personality.
11. Tell teen of your concerns; invite his input, add yours, and integrate into formal contract.

12. Put contract in writing with limits and consequences clearly stated to avoid misunderstanding.

Sample Contract

Frank A. and Shirley B. *Parent* agree with John Q. *Teen* that all family members shall respect and adhere to the following family rules:

1. Participate in family home evening, scripture study, and family prayer.
2. Participate willingly in family activities.
3. Be respectful of family members in speech and in action.
4. Refrain from tobacco, alcohol, and other drugs.
5. Attend church meetings regularly (including seminary, where applicable).

In addition to family rules, *Parents* will be responsible for:

1. Food (except for that purchased during extracurricular activities).
2. Shelter and other physical needs.
3. Clothing agreeable to both parties.
4. Sporting equipment and participation funds.
5. House privileges (including but not limited to the use of the phone, TV, video games, stereo equipment, the car, etc.).
6. Allowance, when earned.
7. Vacations and other family activities.
8. Permission for reasonable individual extracurricular activities.
9. Occasional funding for above activities (as negotiated on a case-by-case basis).

Don't forget to include custom-made rules *important to your teen*. For example:

10. Parents agree not to say bad things about Teen's friends.
11. Parents will not lecture for more than five minutes and then must listen to Teen.
12. Parents will respect Teen's privacy and give him space when he needs it.

In addition to family rules, *Teen* will be responsible for:

1. Obeying curfew.
2. Completing daily chores (dishes, garbage, etc., as assigned).
3. Mowing the lawn and cleaning room on Saturdays.
4. Being responsible for schoolwork and regular attendance.
5. Working part-time to pay for car insurance.
6. Maintaining reasonable personal hygiene.
7. Occasional babysitting (not to exceed one night per week).
8. Cleaning up after self and putting away personal laundry.
9. Being on time for meals.

Don't forget to include custom-made rules that are *important to you*. For example:

10. Teen agrees not to get a tattoo.
11. Teen will listen willingly for five minutes to Parent's input, then gets to respond.
12. Teen will not sneak out at night, etc.

If this contract is violated, the following consequences will apply:

1. For curfew infraction—temporary loss of permission for extracurricular activities.
2. For undone chores—loss of allowance, loss of funding for extracurricular activities.
3. For school infraction—loss of phone, TV, computer, stereo (any or all, depending on severity).
4. For loss of income—no car insurance, no car.
5. Other consequences as needed, keeping them as natural and/or logical as possible.

Penalties for breaking *Family* rules:
Three warnings before "disfellowshipment" occurs. (See p. 77 for a discussion of "disfellowshipment.")

1. First warning—verbal, with long lecture.
2. Second warning—one Saturday of work detail.
3. Third warning—loss of all house privileges for one week.
4. Disfellowshipment—same as number 3 above, but for one month, or until compliance occurs. Additional privileges may be revoked as necessary, such as laundry service, food preparation, use of family supplies, use of private bedroom, etc.

If Teen refuses to respect terms of disfellowshipment, this contract will be mediated by an unbiased third party, and Parent and Teen agree to abide by the negotiated resolution.

_____   _____
PARENT   TEEN

_____
DATE

Remember that this contract is just a prototyp~~e~~
that you and your teen must discuss, negotiate, an~~d~~
upon each and every rule, responsibility, and conseque~~nce~~
during the planning process. You may think that your teen
will be unwilling to negotiate a contract with you, but
when there is much tension in the home, most teens are
willing to take whatever action will make the situation
more tolerable, especially when they know that some of
their pet peeves are also going to be addressed. This is why
it is especially important that you, as parents, actually do
address your teen's particular needs, concerns, and even
complaints, accommodating these when possible and
incorporating them into the finished contract.

In the unlikely event your child *is* unwilling to negotiate a contract, offer an incentive. If no reasonable incentive is effective, tell the teen you are left with no
alternative but to apply the disfellowshipment penalty.
Remember to do these things in a spirit of love and concern.

Letter to a Parent

My Dear Friend:

Thank you for coming over last night and allowing me
to witness the great love you have for your daughter. It is
beautiful to see a mother care so selflessly that she lays
her own feelings and issues aside to love unconditionally.
Parenthood is the hardest calling I've ever had. I know
from experience how painful and difficult it is to watch a
child make such dangerous decisions. The worst part, of
course, is knowing that they have their agency and are
using it to hurt themselves. Sometimes it seemed like
Satan and I were in a tug-of-war for my son's spirit, and I

felt his presence in our home as surely as I saw you sitting in my living room last night.

At first, I played into his hands. I dug in my heels, kicking and screaming to keep from losing that tug-of-war. The more I tried to beat him at his own game of force and control, the more ground he gained. He had all the media and the music and the kids at school and the whole society on his side. I only had myself, because I was using his methods to win, not Heavenly Father's. Of course, I didn't realize that until I had just about lost the battle. Then I finally gave up my own agenda and turned to Him. I admitted my way wasn't working and asked Him to help me do it right. I wanted Heavenly Father to show me how to fix my child His way. The answer I got was one I didn't care for, one that made me feel insecure and out of control. The answer I got was that I couldn't "fix" anyone Heavenly Father's way, because Heavenly Father's way doesn't involve "fixing." He would not allow me to fix my son, because that was not my stewardship. He had given him his agency, and it was his responsibility to fix things for himself.

Don't get me wrong. That didn't mean there was nothing I could do. But there was no sure way I could get my teenage son back on track. Like you said last night, I couldn't just pick him up, say no, and keep him from harm's way like I could when he was little. What I could do was set guidelines, arrange carefully chosen consequences, love him, and pray for him. And by the way, the things that worked best, though I tried them all, were the loving him and the praying for him. I prayed that he would be able to see clearly; that he would be able to remember the goals he had when he came to earth; that he would experience the opportunities, incidents, and people in his life that would give him the best possible chance to choose wisely and well; and that he would be true to the great person he really was and always had been. I prayed that he would feel the love of our family and not lose sight of our teachings.

My battle with Satan was no less real, but now I was fighting smart. I did my best to avoid power struggles with my child. I concentrated on speaking the truth to him with love, instead of fear. When the fear got the better of me and I messed up, I prayed until I could go back, apologize, and do it the right way. I wasn't more lenient; I was just more loving. I wanted to behave in a way that would allow the Spirit to be with me. I stopped obsessing about my child's bad behavior and started concentrating on who he really was and how I could help him remember who he really was. I looked for the positive in him and took every chance I could to point it out, hoping this would remind him of his innate goodness.

It wasn't a quick fix. I wish I could tell you it was. But over time, my son showed his true colors. He showed them because we, in all our imperfection, tried to do it Heavenly Father's way—with gentleness and long suffering and love unfeigned. The time came when he wasn't angry with us anymore, even when we had to punish him. He was in limbo for one and a half years, with no perks, no particular privileges, no driver's license. For a while, we didn't even buy him clothes because we felt he needed to earn his own money and be responsible for his own upkeep insofar as possible since he wasn't complying with our rules. But he was not angry with us because we were able, with a lot of help from Heavenly Father, to apply these agreed-upon, contracted consequences without anger. He knew and felt our love, and even though he didn't agree with our methods, he was able to respect them. We got rid of the power struggle by allowing him his agency and not withdrawing our love or support when he abused it.

I should say that, for a brief period, my son was not expected to comply with the same rules that the other children were upholding—rules he had once lived by. He had become involved in substance abuse and could not be reached on the level he had previously occupied. What had once worked well began to work against us and against him. As he and the family began to deal with his addictions, we had to take a serious look at where he was and come up with a long-range, realistic plan to get him back on track. We realized that because he was operating on a telestial level, he would need to work back to celestial living step by step, with our help. At first, our expectations were more terrestrial than celestial. He had to go into treatment and stop using marijuana. He had to attend school. He had to hold down a job. He had to come home at night, at an agreed-upon time. He had to be honest, even when the news was bad. Probably because of the good feeling we had recaptured, he was also willing to attend church, participate with the family in activities, do his share around the house, and show respect for us as parents.

Our son still had limits and consequences, but they were different in nature. When he gave up marijuana, but chose to continue smoking, we let him know he was choosing other things, too. He was choosing to lose the full fellowship of family status, which involved the loss of care taking, including prepared meals, laundry services, and other family perks. At one point, a Latter-day Saint family counselor suggested that we use tough love measures and force our son to comply with all of our wishes or be ejected from the home. I was not in favor of that and could only foresee using such drastic methods if there were absolutely no other solution. In order for me to justify that kind of action, a young person would have to be completely alienated from his parents' influence and engaged in such dangerous behavior that the hope of his reaching bottom and accepting help was worth the risk of putting him out on the street.

Our son was not in that position; however, we did want to put our collective foot down on some basic issues and reestablish our authority. Because he seemed to be making steady progress under our care, we came up with the idea of, in a sense, "disfellowshipping" him from the family. He was still a part of us, but would no longer be entitled to privileges he had once taken for granted, such as having his laundry done. Our job was to love him back into "full fellowship." His job was to take the steps necessary to make that happen. As we withdrew a privilege, we talked to him about it with love and explained why we felt it was necessary for him to feel that loss. He always knew that we were doing what we did in order to make it uncomfortable for him to continue the behavior he was choosing. It was a complicated, ever-changing contract we had. Sometimes one thing or set of things wouldn't work, so we would meet with him and renegotiate. My husband and I were united in feeling and praying our way toward whatever plan would help get our son back on track. It was step by baby step, all the way.

As a couple, we counseled with each other and devised ways to help our child see the light without pushing him farther away. Much of it came with prayer and inspiration, and I know you will receive the same help. It is important to maintain those strong standards and guidelines for the family and to let the teen know that he or she is violating them, that the violation is unacceptable, and that there will be consequences, some natural, some enforced, for that behavior. But it is also important to still love the child, still laugh with the child, still enjoy the child, so that the very thing you have that has the most ability to pull him back into the fold—his love for you and your family, and through you, the Church, and Heavenly Father—remains intact and even grows.

I know that's easy to say and seems almost impossible to do. I also know that two very weak, imperfect people received the help we needed from our Father in Heaven to do it. I figure if we can, anyone can.

You didn't get what you came for last night. I sense you were looking for a plan—a sure-fire plan that would work, that would keep your child safe. I wish there were one, but I have learned the hard way that there isn't. She will have to make all her decisions for herself, but that doesn't mean there's nothing you can do. Heavenly Father doesn't fix things for us, but look how much He is able to do for us when we get out of His way. He will whisper to you, through the Spirit, what you should do and when you should do it. He will help you formulate and stick to your plan and give you ideas of how to create limits and discipline she can respect and understand. He will help you love her unconditionally if you are willing to let Him; and she will feel that love and be softened. This will not immediately make her decide to do everything you want her to do, but once she can give up fighting you and your authority as parents, she will be able, that much sooner, to listen to that part of herself she is ignoring right now—the part that agrees with you. Right now, she doesn't want to agree with you. It's awful, but that's where she is. And the only way I know this is because we've been there.

Your daughter knows what is right. I believe that. At some level, she knows what is right, because you have taught her. If she feels any part of your love for her is conditional upon her doing what is right, she will keep testing and testing that love until she feels it coming through for her. Offering unconditional love will not control her or make her do what you want, but it will allow her to eventually realize what she wants. I believe that what you want and what she wants will turn out to be one and the same thing—her eternal salvation—but she is clearly one girl who needs to realize this for herself. If she is involved in a tug-of-war with you, she will keep pulling and pulling, because she is not a person who gives up. Unfortunately, while she is pulling, she is concentrating on the struggle. She isn't noticing the rope burns on her hands, or that the ground she's gaining is full of potholes and brackish water. Unconditional love believes in who that person was in the spirit world and helps that person remember who she is and why she came to earth. I remember how hard it is show this kind of love when a child is being openly rebellious. We know, however, that with God all things are possible, and He will help you be a mirror for her, a mirror that reminds her of everything she is and can be.

We didn't always get it right, but when we realized we'd gone wrong, we were always able to repent, go back, repair whatever damage we had done, and move forward. Nobody does it perfectly, but with the Lord's help, you will be able to do the job well. I wish you the best of luck and know you will get the inspiration and personal revelation you need. If there's anything I can do, anything at all, let me know. I had so much help from other parents in my ward. I don't know what your plan should be because it has to fit your personalities and family structure, but I did get pretty good at discovering (sometimes the hard way) what worked and what didn't, so if you get to a point where you are making that plan and you want someone to bounce it off of, I'd be glad to listen and see if I can get a feel for whether it would work or not. We must have tried just about everything at one point or another, and if our track record can save you some time and keep you from going down any blind alleys, we'd be glad to talk to you.

You are a great person, and if anyone can help her through this, you can. She's lucky to have all that power and strength concentrated in her direction. My prayers are with both of you.

With much love,

Your friend

7

THE THREE R's:
REALITY, RESPECT, AND
RELATIONSHIP

YOU'VE REACHED A milestone with the formulation of a workable plan. The "three R's": reality, respect, and relationship, will play a major role as you prepare to put that plan into action. Why is a hearty dose of reality so invaluable to a teenager in the throes of rebellion? Because one of our most significant contributions, as parents, is to keep telling it like it is. The success of any plan we make depends upon our willingness to enforce it one hundred percent, providing honest feedback as needed.

If we will resist the temptation to sidestep conflict by glossing over unacceptable actions or activities, we can avoid enabling our teens to misbehave. This is certain to make a few waves, but anything less would be selling them short. We need to look into their eyes and speak frankly, facing problems head-on as they arise. By acting as mirrors for our children, we make it possible for them to view their behavior more clearly, along with its effects and consequences. As we refuse to allow them to kid themselves, or us, we teach them accountability. There is nothing more powerful than telling the truth without equivocation.

When a teen is having difficulties, we should resist the impulse to cover for him. We don't want to violate his privacy by giving out personal information or sharing confidences, but neither should we hide the fact that he is struggling. Honesty is the best policy, and modeling it is our responsibility. Being genuine will help a child connect with others and get the support and assistance he needs.

> Sister Horton was a single mother whose husband had died when her children were quite young. She had been living in the same home for years, and her faithful ward had been supportive of her efforts to raise four small children on her own. Home teachers had given blessings, performed baptisms, and been "stand-in" dads for Scout outings and daddy-daughter dances. Things had not been easy for Sister Horton, but she knew the ward was behind her, and her devotion to the children had earned their love and approval.

As the teenage years began, this mother of four redoubled her efforts to be a strength in the lives of her children. She was proud of them and let them know that what they did mattered to her and reflected on the family. She taught family home evening lessons that were both timely and uplifting, and she expected her children to continue choosing what was right. For the most part, her expectations were fulfilled. The oldest son became an Eagle Scout and eventually left on a mission. His brother, an excellent athlete, won a scholarship to BYU and became a strong member of the track team. Sister Horton was grateful that her sons had done so well without the influence of a father and frequently thanked members of the ward for their involvement with the family.

These positive experiences left Sister Horton totally unprepared for the turmoil she felt when her youngest daughter tearfully disclosed that she had seen her older sister smoking a cigarette in the backyard. Completely devastated by the news, Sister Horton confronted her daughter immediately about this behavior, telling her in no uncertain terms that smoking was not only bad for her health, but spiritually disastrous. She warned that if the experimentation did not stop, the privilege of driving the old Volkswagen Bug would.

Of course, this particular daughter assured her mother that there would be no more smoking. Perhaps she meant it, too, but curiosity and peer pressure got the better of her, and she not only continued the smoking, but formed a regular habit. Sister Horton, to her credit, knew that her daughter had not complied with the agreement they had made. She could smell the smoke every time her daughter walked into the room. Ultimately, various consequences were enforced, but nothing seemed to deter the girl's behavior.

Sister Horton was beside herself. She couldn't stop worrying about her daughter's safety and well-being. And if cigarettes weren't bad enough, she had read that they were the gateway to marijuana and other drugs. What could be worse than that? Over and over again, Sister Horton tried to figure out where she had gone wrong in raising her daughter. Somehow she had let her down; in fact, she had let the whole ward down. It would be terrible if they knew that this beautiful girl they had helped teach and nurture had turned her back on all of them and gone against everything they believed in. What would they think of her? What would they think of the whole Horton family?

This is where Sister Horton made a decision that separated her from the very love and support she needed. She resolved to keep her daughter's difficulties from ward members, no matter what the cost. Instead of turning to them for assistance as she had in the past, she shut them out and pretended all was well. The sad thing is, the ward knew all was not well. Many families had children in the high school, and it was no secret that this girl was having problems.

Some tried to approach Sister Horton to see if they could help, but she was too fearful of their judgment, or too caught up in self-judgment, to let them in. Over time, they quit trying, becoming more and more uncomfortable as they sensed but were not allowed to share her distress.

As the daughter wandered farther and farther off the right path, ward members who had lost intimate contact with the family felt awkward around her. It had been made clear to them that they couldn't address this situation directly, so they began to look the other way and not address it at all. What were they supposed to do for this girl who was so obviously troubled? How could they be open and connect with her when the family was so resistant? What were they supposed to say? It wasn't long before they said nothing. The girl, not surprisingly, noticed their avoidance and used it to justify the things she was doing wrong. She would often tell her mother how phony the church people were and that they thought they were too good for her. She called them hypocrites and said her nonmember friends and their parents were more loving and Christlike than the ward members.

She did stay marginally active, but this young woman's resentment toward the Church grew. Even her mother's testimony was shaken as she struggled to maintain appearances and wondered at the ward's behavior. She remembered when the ward had been so good at filling her cup and wondered why now she was always coming up empty.

I am not suggesting that Sister Horton, or any of us, should run around the ward broadcasting intimate details of a teenager's behavior and psyche. This would be a complete invasion of his privacy. What I am suggesting is that this ward's hands were tied to some extent, first, by their ignorance and second, by Sister Horton's refusal to come out in the open. They followed her lead, and everyone ended up getting lost. Also lost was the strength that comes when a ward and its members are united in purpose. What were those words of Paul's to the besieged Thessalonians? "Wherefore comfort yourselves together, and edify one another" (1 Thessalonians 5:11).

The second "R" we will talk about is respect. This quality cannot exist without trust, for trust provides the foundation upon which mutual respect is built. When that trust is compromised, as is often the case between parents and teenagers in crisis, the entire relationship is in jeopardy. At this point, the best course is to talk about the loss of trust openly, setting up some ground rules for reestablishing good faith over time. Our children need our respect, which is why earning back trust is crucial.

During my internship, I saw families in which teenagers had violated their parents' belief in them so many times there was no trust at all—and for good reason. I was always amazed to see how those very teenagers who had abused their parents' faith would try to turn things around and make their parents feel guilty about not trusting them. Some parents, shell-shocked by recent events, were pulled into this trap. In these cases, we were encouraged to make bold statements to the teenagers, letting them know, without equivocation, that they deserved not to be trusted; that they had, in fact, earned their parents' mistrust and would now have to take responsibility for earning back the trust they had lost. We went on to say that earning it back would not be easy and might require weeks, even months of good behavior.

We learned to empower parents to honor their personal experience, respecting the need for time in rebuilding trust that has been violated by a child. Both the parents and the child should understand that rebuilding is and should be the teenager's responsibility. Children who have broken faith need to accept that responsibility, along with their parents' personal time frames for recovery. How quickly a parent will trust again depends on many things, including early childhood dynamics, and cannot be dictated.

Of course, parents must be honest and trustworthy too. If we have been inconsistent or hypocritical in the past, here's our chance to admit it, apologize, and turn over a new leaf. In this case, we would have a responsibility for rebuilding as well, but that responsibility would be separate and apart from our teen's. Our responsibility should not be allowed to dilute or diminish our teen's responsibility. Allowing children to use parental issues to avoid their own is never helpful. If, on the other hand, our past and present actions have already gained the trust of our teens, why not demand the respect that goes with it? We can use the power of being a trustworthy, respected person to strengthen our child and influence him for good.

Trust is a peculiar thing. When trust is merited, receiving it builds character and increases self-esteem. On the other hand, receiving undeserved trust has a corrupting effect, compromising integrity and undermining self-love. We must not get caught in the trap of trusting teenagers who have become untrustworthy. Not only does it jeopardize their well-being, but it reinforces the very behaviors they are trying to hide. If we extend undeserved trust, it will block us from supplying the help that is desperately needed. Confronting dishonest teenagers with their own untrustworthiness can put them solidly on the road to reclaiming their self-respect. Anything less is cowardice: giving in to our own inability or unwillingness to face the truth, tell the truth, and demand the truth. Let's take a look at two other families who encountered the same issue the Hortons did, teen smoking.

Brother Gonzalez had been worried about his only daughter for months. She was growing up fast and had entered the age of cars and parties and curfews. She was a pretty good kid, but lately she had been less respectful and seemed more inclined to challenge family rules and parental authority. He knew all teens went through this, or so he had been told, but Brother Gonzalez couldn't help feeling uneasy, especially now that she often came into the house smelling of cigarettes.

Of course, she always assured him that neither she nor any of her good friends were smoking and explained that because there were clouds of smoke in the air at high school parties, it naturally got on her clothes. If Brother

Gonzalez questioned her further, his daughter would become defensive. "What's the matter, Dad, don't you trust me?" she would say. "I can't believe you actually think I'm smoking. I might as well be doing it if you're going to blame me anyway!" These words made her father feel guilty. Certainly he should trust his daughter. People needed and deserved to be trusted, and besides, when people were trusted they rose to the occasion. It was like a self-fulfilling prophecy. Believe the worst and you'll get the worst. Believe the best and you'll get the best. He thought of how he would feel if someone didn't believe him—angry and misunderstood. If she got into that frame of mind, she would really be vulnerable to smoking. Right then, Brother Gonzalez decided to show his daughter that he had faith in her. He would help her feel good about herself and her family by proving how much she was loved and trusted.

Over the next few weeks, Brother Gonzalez did his best to quiet his fears and reassure his daughter that she was trusted. Sometimes this was easier than others. There were nights when she would walk into the house and the smell of cigarettes was overpowering. A couple of times he tried to question her gently and lovingly, but she immediately labeled his concern as lack of trust and began bristling with indignation. Brother Gonzalez, in turn, would feel guilty for doubting her. He would remind himself that his daughter had never been a liar and that she could never seem so hurt and offended if she were indeed smoking. In fact, he would tell himself, this girl simply could not be smoking. She knew what was right, and she knew smoking was wrong.

With that, the cycle would begin again. She would assure him she wasn't smoking; he would feel relieved and sorry for doubting her. Sometimes, for a while, she would come in without the telltale odor. Other times, she would smell like chewing gum or lemon juice. Eventually, though, she would come in smelling like smoke. Taking his "trust" for granted, she would grow careless. Assaulted by evidence, his fears would begin to return. Not wanting to accuse her unfairly, he became more and more adept at pushing those fears down without questioning her, avoiding the inevitable confrontations, while always feeling guilty for not trusting his own daughter.

Unfortunately, Brother Gonzalez's daughter *was* smoking, and his misplaced trust was clearly detrimental to his daughter's well-being. With the best of intentions and much love, he had failed to meet her needs.

Her girlfriend, on the other hand, met with a different situation at home. She, too, came into the house smelling of smoke each night. Her parents, the Masons, had seen their daughter make many good decisions in her life, but they couldn't help feeling concerned. Was there a possibility she could be smoking? It seemed unbelievable, yet the Masons, who had already raised a few children, were convinced that it was never safe to say "never" when dealing with adolescents. Taking this into consideration, they questioned her in some detail. Her reaction was similar to her friend's—she became defensive and accused her parents of not trusting her. These parents, who had been around the block a few more times than Brother Gonzalez, let their daughter know that they did trust her and would continue to trust her until and unless she gave them reason not to. Smelling so strongly of smoke was, they went on, reason to be suspicious, and it was because of their trust in her that they were not jumping to any conclusions. In fact, they wanted her to understand that their instinct was to believe her, regardless of the sensory evidence.

Mom and Dad ended the conversation by letting her know they were concerned about the behavior that was going on around her and that they would be watching her carefully and monitoring her activities closely. No one was immune to temptation, and they intended to do everything possible to support her in continuing to make good choices. These parents reminded their daughter that her resolve could only be strengthened by knowing they were actively involved in sustaining the boundaries she had set for herself. They also suggested, since she had made it clear she was determined not to be a smoker, that it might be helpful to get together with her best buddies and plan some smoke-free parties and activities. It would be easier to hold the line that way, and it wouldn't hurt to avoid all that secondhand smoke either! And maybe some of the other kids would be glad for a chance to breathe some clean air, too.

The Masons, who were not convinced their daughter had done anything wrong, were letting her know that only her actions could destroy their trust. At the same time, they let her know that they were committed, informed parents who would not be hiding their heads in the sand, but would be actively guarding, guiding, and governing her. They were not going to be emotionally blackmailed into wearing blinders, but would be as open and above-board about their concerns and interests as they hoped she would be about her actions and activities. In other words, they were dealing in truth and would act and react accordingly.

The parents' position modeled respect for themselves and for their daughter, creating an environment that benefited everyone concerned. By the way, this young woman *was not* using cigarettes, though she had placed herself in some risky situations, an issue which was addressed on an ongoing basis. Had she been smoking, appropriate action would have been taken. These parents were laying a foundation of truth and knew that meaningful trust could not be built without mutual respect.

Another way we can show respect for teens is by validating their feelings. Many of us prefer to ignore or discount our children's feelings, because they make us too uncomfortable. Often, they bring to light feelings of our own, feelings we would rather forget. Denying our children's experience, or colluding with them in hiding important reactions to real situations in their lives, is disrespectful and makes intimacy impossible.

> One of my children has a learning disability that can make school frustrating and difficult. I used to help her differently than I do now. In the old days, I would try to cheer her up immediately when she was feeling down about her difficulties. I just couldn't stand to see her feeling discouraged, so I'd begin by listing all the successful people who had ever had learning disabilities. Then I would move into a dissertation on how lucky she was to have such good intelligence to help her cope. To lighten the mood, I'd follow with some well-aimed jokes about the teacher or subject that was troubling her. I would generally close by reminding her that everyone has a cross to bear and that all of us grow from mastering the challenges in our lives.

I'm not saying that any of this was wrong, or even that my old methods don't have their place. I have realized, however, that my daughter's feelings also have their place, a very important one. Instead of trying to avoid her feelings and the feelings they engender in me, I now try to listen to and validate them. When I am strong enough to listen and to respect her experience, she is able to move through her sadness and make room for her natural optimism. I become not only a sounding board, but a dumping place. As I am more willing to allow her feelings, she is more willing and able to deal with them constructively. Once she has been able to vent, she is often the one who is then ready to start problem-solving. What great power teenagers have to heal themselves, if we will only let them, and hear them.

The best tool for helping a teenager get back on track is the power of influence and persuasion that comes from a good, loving, open relationship. Until feelings can be shared in a safe, nonthreatening environment, where everyone is free to speak, that kind of relationship will not be developed. This is not to say that teenage tantrums or manipulative histrionics should be indulged in the name of self-expression. There is a difference between respecting honest feelings and encouraging manipulations that are in no way constructive. We can acknowledge and validate a child's anger, for example, without allowing him to direct it at us, or condoning inappropriate behavior. Honoring our own feelings is every bit as crucial as honoring our children's in establishing and maintaining a healthy relationship.

This brings us to the final "R"—relationship. Even in the midst of a parent-teen crisis, steps can be taken to build the relationship. It is absolutely possible to give love while withholding approval. We can enforce consequences and yet be loving, even empathic. Fun can still be had by two people who are having difficulties, as long as those difficulties are not allowed to fester. Need some ideas? How about renting one of those *Dumb and Dumber* movies they're all so fond of, forgetting you're an adult and giggling like a kid again? Or if that doesn't suit you, why not challenge your sulky teen to a wrestling match, a water-balloon bust, or a food fight? Write him a cute note, draw funny pictures on it, make him a photo album with pictures of you together in happier days. The child you knew before he became a teenager is still there. All you have to do is connect with the part of him that is hibernating behind all those hormones.

Some of our teenagers may have said or done terrible things to us and to themselves. We can continue to love them, and they can continue to feel that love, if we are able to show it. Of course we get angry. Here is an opportunity to pray for assistance in releasing that anger and moving to forgiveness. We might even try praying that our teens will forgive us! Some parents report that calling a trusted friend and venting a little can ease things. Others find relief in writing about strong feelings, or working them out at the gym. Whatever path we choose, we need to keep our own feelings moving so we don't get stuck in negativity and spoil those valuable relationships with our children.

HELPS AND HINTS

Letter to a Teen

My Dear Young Friend:

We talked last night about agency, and it's true that you do have yours. In her heart, your mom knows that and so do I. I have learned it the hard way, as a parent, and she is learning it now. You are teaching her one of the most difficult and painful things parents have to learn— that their children must and will choose for themselves. It would be easier and safer for parents to be able to force their children to do the right things, just like it would have been easier to come to earth using Satan's plan. But as you know, Satan's plan was not Heavenly Father's plan. He preferred to allow His children to make their own choices and to grow and learn from their own mistakes.

Your mother cannot stop you from smoking. That's a no-brainer. And Heavenly Father *will* not stop you from smoking. He will not, because He knows that the only way your stopping will mean anything as far as your eternal growth goes is if *you* decide to stop. You are the one who will have to make that choice, and you are the one who will have to go through the withdrawal. You are the one who will crave cigarettes until your addiction goes away, and you are the one who will have to find positive ways to fill the need that smoking fills for you.

Let me run one more thing by you. There is one person who *will* take your agency away from you, if you let him. I think you know that I am talking about our other brother, the one who likes to use force to bring about the results he wants. In heaven, he wanted to force us to be good. He lost that battle, and now he wants to prove that he was right—that we can't make good choices on our own. He wants to prove to Heavenly Father and himself that his plan of force was the best one. He wants to show that in order to be good, we needed to be forced—that we couldn't do it on our own—that we wouldn't be strong enough to withstand temptation and stand firmly for what is right and true. Of course, the only way he can do that is to get us to make wrong choices, choices that will mess up our mission here on earth.

We are all going to make wrong choices in our lives. We have our agency, and Heavenly Father allows us to use it. You are using yours every time you light up a cigarette. The interesting thing is that every time you use your agency to make that choice, you lose your agency. That is how Satan works. He tricks us with things that seem like we are exercising free choice. He is so clever that he can often keep us from realizing that his kind of free choice has an aftereffect. As you use your agency, you lose your agency. Every time you light up a cigarette and have that particular kind of fun and good feeling, you are giving up your agency—because you are creating and strengthening an addictive process. If and when you finally decide that you care enough about yourself, both body and spirit, to quit smoking, you will realize how much freedom you have given up with every drag on a cigarette. Every inhalation of smoke and nicotine increases your addiction and makes it more difficult to choose not to smoke. Maybe you've already noticed how difficult it is to quit, how much the desire for nicotine messes with your mind.

My hope is that you won't let a desire for that kind of pleasure rule you. There is no one on earth, smoker or nonsmoker, who can deny the scientific evidence that smoking causes cancer. It's a fact. Adult smokers will tell you that they started as teens when they weren't particularly paying attention to the consequences. By the time they got to be adults and realized that health doesn't last forever, they had often become so hooked that they couldn't stop. Most adult smokers would love to stop. Unfortunately, they have given up so much of their agency, given up so much of themselves to nicotine and addiction, that they cannot, or at least they believe they cannot, which pretty much amounts to the same thing. I have counseled these people in therapy, and they feel as if they have lost control over their lives. They used their agency to smoke, or to use drugs, or to gamble, or to do whatever addictive behavior they chose and in doing so, lost the ability to use their agency to stop the behavior.

Let me just add that the percentage of young people who use cigarettes and stop there is extremely small. In other words, those who smoke, will likely toke. These powerful substances alter your neurochemistry—the chemicals in your brain—and take you out of control. Of course, Satan is glad to do his part, too.

None of us came to this earth to fail. We believed in ourselves, or we would not have come. If we had not been willing to risk everything to prove that we were strong enough, we would not be here. We would have sided with Satan. Instead, we chose to use our agency to take a body, come to earth, and learn how to control it. We were and are spirits first. Our spirits are supposed to control our bodies. When we choose to smoke, or drink, or eat too much, we are allowing our bodies to rule our spirits. That is like being in a car, pushing on the accelerator, and allowing it to steer itself. I think you can imagine what a wild ride that would be and how much chance you would have of coming out of that ride without serious injury. If you drove that way often enough, the car would be totaled. In other words, because your spirit knows what is best, it isn't a good idea to let your body make too many of the decisions.

Well, there's my teaching moment, for what it's worth. Even as I am writing this, I am aware that you have to learn your own things your own way. Your parents, others who love you, and I wish you could learn the easy way, just by our telling you, but it doesn't seem to work like that. People have to learn for themselves in the ways they feel most comfortable. All I can do is tell you my experience, and you get to decide whether it means anything to you. I would also like to share a little bit of my son's experience. I want you to know that I don't share this without his permission. Before he left on his mission, I asked if he would mind my using our experience in talking to young women. He said that would be fine, so here goes.

My son started out smoking cigarettes and ended up smoking marijuana—lots of it. He totally enjoyed these things and had no desire to quit whatsoever. We tried to make him quit, but it didn't work; in fact, he just used more. That was his choice, just as it was our job to try to influence him to make better decisions. Eventually, things happened to him. He had a really frightening experience with drugs. He had some big disappointments with friends who let him down because they cared more about drugs than they cared about him. That tends to happen with chemical dependency. He started not caring about things that he used to love, like basketball. He flunked out of school. He lost sight of himself. One night, after a party, he broke through his own addictive process and saw clearly what was happening to himself and his life. It was as if he took the wheel of his car for a minute and finally saw where he was headed. That was when he came into our room and asked his father for a priesthood blessing. When he realized he was in trouble and needed help, the first thing he asked for was a priesthood blessing. He had been telling himself, and us, that he didn't really believe the Church was true any more, but actions speak louder than words, and when he was frightened and lost, it was to Heavenly Father he turned. I tell you this because he now feels that his testimony was never really gone. It was just covered over by worldly pleasures—by cigarettes and pot and music and other things. I guess you could say it sort of went into hibernation. But when the sun came out, so did his testimony—and that's what got him through.

It was a long and difficult road back, and he wishes he hadn't traveled down it. He paid a big price for those cigarettes that started his journey and so did our family. All of us were hurt and though he wasn't too torn up by it at the time, he is now. Now that he is back in the driver's seat, he remembers that wild ride and regrets hurting us. In fact, I think that is the hardest thing for him. But he also regrets hurting himself. He regrets that he lost sight of his goals and barely graduated from high school. He regrets that he lost sight of basketball—one of his greatest loves—and never got to play on the high school team. He watches his brothers and realizes that he lost a period of his life that was supposed to be a learning process. He lost the wholesome, innocent fun they're having because he gave it up for a chemical—something false—fake fun. What he traded for that fake fun was his self-esteem and his self-respect. Yes, he's won that back, but it wasn't easy. It was painful. By the time he stopped using, things had changed about his personality. The chemical had left its mark on him, and he had a lot of work to do getting himself and his life back on track. Substance abuse counselors will tell you that people who use addictive substances become liars, and my son would tell you that too. They start by lying to themselves, pretending they are in control, and they end up lying to others. Relationships are damaged, and people lose trust in them. Worst of all, they lose trust in themselves. All they trust is the next cigarette, the next drink, the next bowl.

I see you looking down that same road he traveled. You are too good for that road, and so was he. I couldn't stop him from going down it, and I can't stop you from going down it. All I can do is tell you what happened to us, to our family. I hope when you look down that road you will take the time to look at all the things that are on it. I know it looks good because Satan is great at camouflage, but there are a lot of rocks and thorns and potholes that you have to look carefully to see. Maybe you can learn from his experience. I know my other children have. They watched him go down that road, so they've seen it up close and personal. They know the whole story, not just the part that Satan wants them to see. Telling you about it isn't the same as living it like we did, and I know that. But telling is all I can do, so I have. What you do with it is up to you.

I'm sorry this letter is so long, and if you have actually read this far I thank you. I thank you for giving me a chance to say what I need to say. I hope you will be able to give your parents a chance to say what they need to say too. You can help them by telling them the way you can stand to listen to them most.

And so I end by telling you the same thing I told you at the beginning. You have your agency. I hope you will make the choices that allow you to keep that agency. But whatever choices you make, I want you to know that your parents, your Young Women leaders, and I love and care about you. We are not here to judge you. That's not our job. Our job is to guide you as best we can, and your job is to take all the information available to you and make the best decision you can make for yourself. I do urge you to keep going to church and attending Young Women's. Even if you aren't convinced of the truthfulness of the gospel, many people you love are convinced of it, and maybe you should at least keep an open mind just in case they're right. Also, make sure that you are true to all the parts of yourself. I know that most of you wants to smoke right now, but there is a part that isn't so sure that's the right decision. I hope you will honor that part too. Balance the input that goes into your life so you can make an informed decision. Balance the spiritual and the physical so you don't put all your eggs in one basket. It might turn out to be the wrong one.

I believed in my son, and I believe in you. I have heard you bear your testimony, and the Spirit was with you. I felt it. Remember that when you are smoking, the Spirit is unable to be with you in your decision-making process. Just as you are experimenting with cigarettes, I hope you will experiment on the word by praying, reading the scriptures, and attending church meetings. If you will allow yourself to keep your options open, I think your own strong spirit will not let you down. My guess is that, in the end, your spirit will win out over your body and say, "Leave the driving to me, buddy." You came to earth for a reason, and I don't see you letting Satan or anyone else mess you up, at least not for long.

Love,

Your Friend

Love and Lighthouses

If you make the Lord your lighthouse,
He will guide your passage through
every shallow, rocky channel
till the harbor is in view.
And the ship that is your spirit
will not sink in any storm,
for His love will be the beacon
that will keep you safe and warm.

8

MOVING FORWARD: PUTTING YOUR PLAN INTO ACTION

NOW THAT WE'VE discussed keeping our teens based in reality, respecting them and being respected by them, and strengthening our relationships, we are ready to put those carefully constructed parenting plans into action. One of the most important things we will do to enhance our children's well-being is to administer these plans in an atmosphere of love and goodwill. This will also be one of the most difficult things we do.

Every time we enforce a consequence, we are painfully aware that limits have been ignored, boundaries overstepped. Common reactions might be anger, fear, disappointment, hurt, even a sense of betrayal. It is both useful and appropriate to express these feelings to our teens, but that expression should be made rationally, in as even-handed a manner as possible.

Confronting a child in the heat of passion can be counterproductive. It is perfectly acceptable to say "I'm too upset to talk about this right now," as long as the discussion is still timely. We may choose to make an appointment later the same day, or even "sleep on it." In the meantime, we can spend some time with our feelings. How do we do that? A review of Chapter 2 might spark some ideas, but ideas are only helpful when put into action. Write in a journal, call a friend, bang a drum! Do whatever it is that nurtures you and gets those feelings worked out.

When my son was at the height of his terrible teens, sometimes I would feel so angry I just wanted to shake him. How could he make such decisions, I would think; we taught him better than this. Look at all the love we and our extended family have given him, and he is just throwing it back in our faces. No—worse than that, he's taking advantage of it. He knows he can be just as rotten as he wants, and everyone will still love him anyway. Where does he get off? At the most difficult times, these are the thoughts that would run through my head.

It won't surprise you to hear that I did a lot better at communicating with him and got a lot farther when I took care of some of my anger before we got together. My best outlet was calling up one of my sisters and really letting him have it for a few minutes. To her, I could rant and rave and know that nothing I said was going to inflict injury. I also knew I could trust her not to judge my son, or me. Letting off some steam in this way always helped me regain my perspective. When I was finished, I would usually be laughing as I realized how out of proportion my stored-up feelings had become. Now I was free to experience the deep love and concern I felt for my child and act accordingly.

Of course, the best comfort available, as always, came and will come from our Heavenly Father. I never went to Him with a sorrow that couldn't be softened, or a pain that couldn't be soothed. He does know how to heal the wounded heart. He also knows how to watch His children make mistakes and still find ways to be loving. Surely He will help us do the same.

With Heavenly Father's guidance and having done what we can to restore our emotional and spiritual balance, we will feel worthy and prepared to exercise our plan, addressing all issues constructively. We can invite the Spirit to be with us as we hold our teenagers accountable for their behavior. We should begin by making a clear statement of each infraction, along with its previously assigned consequence. By referring specifically to the written or verbal contract made earlier, we hold our teens accountable for violating that agreement. Many teens will respond by arguing, cajoling, or attempting to reopen contract negotiations. We should do our best, within reason, to listen objectively to their words; their feelings should be heard and respected. In all but the most unusual circumstances, however, teenagers are best served when we stand firm, unswayed by their discomfiture at being held responsible for their actions. We may begin to feel sorry for them as they contemplate the effects of their poor choices. That's okay, as long as we use that sympathy to empathize, not rationalize. Empathy is about love and support; rationalization stems from weakness and indecision. Strong parents can anchor children who find themselves adrift in the world. If we are not resolute in administering these plans, their power to uplift and sustain will be lost. Weak swimmers require life jackets, not pool toys. Our teens deserve only the best gifts—not necessarily what they ask for, but what they need.

Parenting is always a challenge, but parents—even separated or divorced ones—with available, involved partners have a natural advantage because there are two of them. Maintain the united front you have established during the "Making a Plan" phase of this journey. Teens seem to have a special talent for the "divide and conquer" strategy and will use it instinctively when backed into a corner. Knowing and expecting this particular tactic is at least half the battle. We must prepare ourselves as parents to hold our alliance together. When we disagree, we should choose an appropriate time to work out our differences in private, returning to the conference table with whatever compromise is necessary to execute our plan.

Sometimes circumstances change and parents or children feel the need to renegotiate. Perhaps our children feel they should be rewarded for maturing or changing. Maybe they have proven they can be trusted with a little more freedom and would like to discuss adjusting some of their limits. Where considerable growth has taken place, limits may have been assimilated so well that the contract has become obsolete. In this event, drawing up a new contract with raised expectations is often appropriate. On the other hand, if your teenager is not honoring his agreement, or his behavior is deteriorating, it may be necessary to renegotiate the contract with terms that incorporate some tough love measures. If this is the case, it might be useful to meet with a professional, or enlist the aid of an unbiased third party to help mediate. Trusted friends, youth leaders, and church leaders are potential resources for this kind of assistance.

Every effort should be made to sustain a friendship

with our children, especially during hard times. Conflict is unavoidable, but parents who keep their wits about them can handle it constructively. When we are disappointed in our children, it is more effective to empathize than to criticize. We can acknowledge their areas of weakness and validate that improvement is difficult. We can also assure them of our confidence in their ability to turn weakness to strength, with Heavenly Father's help. When children are disappointed in us, we can listen to them and try to understand. We might even find and acknowledge an area of weakness in ourselves.

At times we will want to climb up on a soap box and preach to our teens. We would do well to avoid this urge. Yes, it is our responsibility to provide children with information and guidance, and we should do so. A two-hour sermon, however, is not likely to get the job done. A better strategy might be to spend ten quality minutes and call it a day. The message is more likely to be heard. Of course, some of us get so caught up in worrying about our teens' behavior that we can't stop ourselves. If that is the case, try writing letters. Letters are self-limiting, and many young people prefer them to lectures.

If only speech will satisfy, parents might consider putting a "listening for ten minutes each day to whatever Mom and Dad feel the need to tell me" clause in their contract. Most teens will get a kick out of this, particularly with a little humor thrown in. Laughing with them about how "buggy" parents are can do much to ease the tension. In fact, laughing with them about anything can do much to ease the tension. We might even want to share some stories about when we were teenagers, letting them know we remember what it feels like. Once we have connected in this way, they will be far more open to understanding that we take our responsibilities as parents seriously because we love them and don't want to let them down. Our attentions may drive them crazy at times, but on a deeper level they are fed by the knowledge that we will never give up on them. Our predictability and consistency creates order and safety in their world.

At one point in his recovery, our son let us know that we were "too concerned" about him. We were ridiculous, cared too much, worried too much, made it too hard for him to live the life he wanted to live. He loved us, but we were annoying, in fact, more than annoying. We were a total pain. It was interesting to see his point of view change as we attended a large meeting once a week with several families who were dealing with the same problems we were. It wasn't long before our son realized that many of those families were living with far more serious issues than he could have imagined. He observed that many of the parents were unable to guide their children because they, themselves, had no idea of what was right and what was wrong. Some were alcoholics, a few were abusive, and several had kicked their children out, or were in the process of kicking their children out of their homes. There were parents who had lied to their children so many times that the children could no longer believe anything they said. Others made promises that were never kept. Most seemed unable to set and enforce limits and consequences.

All of these observations were made by our son in the course of group therapy, where he got a chance to see how some of these other families operated. Not all the families, of course, were unhealthy, and there were more than a couple that he admired, but for the first time in his life he was intimately exposed to a number of parents who truly did not know how to love their children in a meaningful way. He saw parents who had abdicated their role completely and came to appreciate the fact that his own parents, though flawed, were reliable, trustworthy people. He could count on us. He had known that before, but had taken it for granted. Now he began to recognize the value of parents that "never gave up." He probably didn't like our methods any better, and I'm sure we still annoyed him, but something in his manner changed after we attended those meetings. There was a certain respect and appreciation that was always present, even during times of disagreement and conflict. He could count on us, and he gradually made it clear that we could count on him.

It comes as no surprise that consistency is central to the success of our parenting plans. This attribute is important in both the enforcement of consequences and the attitude used to enforce them. When we are consistent we build trust, encourage new patterns and expectations, and take ourselves out of the power struggle. As we continue to establish boundaries for our children, we weave a kind of safety net for them, a net they will come to understand, perhaps even value. Such weaving should be done in the right spirit, a spirit of benevolence and compassion wherein an increase of love is freely given and received. This is no easy task, and we will not always do it well, but we can certainly recognize our errors when we fall short, admit them to our children, and apologize sincerely. Again, we do not have to be perfect. It isn't even expected. What we are responsible for is behaving honorably—modeling reliability, accountability, and integrity. That is what we need from our children, and that is what our children need from us. If we would like them to follow our lead, we must try to be consistent in providing a positive example and in humbly admitting our shortcomings when that positive example falters. Being a good parent is not about doing everything right. It is about doing the best we can, acknowledging our mistakes, and trying not to repeat them. That is all Heavenly Father asks of us, and that is all we should ask of ourselves and our children.

HELPS AND HINTS

SUGGESTION: ORGANIZING A SUPPORT GROUP FOR PARENTS OF TEENS

Proposed Topics
1. Stewardship, Not Ownership (reexamining our calling as parents)
2. You're Only a Phone Call Away (accessing spiritual help)
3. To Know You Is to Love You (strengthening relationships with our teens)
4. But, Mom, I Don't *Want* to Be "Peculiar" (supporting Church standards)
5. Hold That Line, but Don't Forget the Cheerleaders! (on disciplining with love)
6. Straight from the Horses' Mouths (what our teens want to tell us)
7. Mayday . . . Mayday (taking care of and getting help for ourselves)
8. United We Stand (parents working together and supporting one another)

M is for the many things you've told me.
O is for the other things you've told me.
T is for the thousands of things you've told me.
H is for the hundreds of things you've told me.
E is for every little thing you've ever told me.
R is for the repeated times you've told me.
Put them all together and they spell . . .
NAG! NAG! NAG!

> Author Unknown

F is for a few things you have shown me.
A is for all of the things you've shown me.
T is for the thousands of things you've shown me.
H is for the hundreds of things you've shown me.
E is for every major thing you've ever shown me.
R is for the repeated times you've shown me.
Put them all together, and they spell . . .
SHOW-OFF! SHOW-OFF! SHOW-OFF!

> Author Un(willing to be)known

9

WHEN THE CHIPS ARE DOWN: DRUGS AND DEPRESSION

A Word about Drugs

FOR THOSE OF YOU who are already fighting this battle and know it, I offer my deep love and respect. There is nothing more devastating than losing your child, even temporarily, to substance abuse. There is certainly nothing more frightening. May you find strength, as many of us do, in the knowledge that victory can be won and is most often witnessed by parents who are informed, dedicated, and prayerful. The majority of teenagers, given the right opportunities, will come off conquerors. Remember, these are the valiant ones, and we can either arm them and ourselves for battle or fall back and surrender to defeat. It's hard to accept, but we cannot guarantee their future. As usual, we can only do what parents can do, but parents should take heart in knowing that we can do quite a lot.

Drugs are increasingly common in the world today, and many parents are naive about the signs and symptoms of this menace. The list at the end of this chapter can be used to identify teenagers who might be involved with drugs. Because we want to believe our children are okay, it is all too easy to dismiss these symptoms as the usual teenage angst. Parents who have serious concerns about their teens and substance abuse would do well to assume those teens are using and go from there. We would all rather err on the side of caution. It takes courage to avoid denial in these circumstances, but we need to remember that parents in denial are parents who cannot help.

Satan has a great tool in the latter days. Before the advent of drugs, it probably took him years to break down a young person's good character, particularly when that young person came from a solid family background. Today, with one smoke, toke, or pill, a teenager can be set firmly on the road to spiritual ruin. Within the space of a school year, or even a semester, a child can go from an honest, responsible student to a rebellious truant who is interested in no one and nothing but the next high. How many times do we see star athletes drop off sports teams or successful students suspended or expelled for habitually cutting class? What happens to previously held standards of chastity when decisions are made under the influence of chemicals? Our youth are in danger, and we need to educate ourselves and each other or many will be lost. Are we doing all we can to make a difference?

There are great treatment programs available in most areas. Local schools are usually the best resource for referrals. Some are funded for on-campus treatment, while others affiliate with off-campus organizations. If in-house treatment is required, the school counselor has usually had experience with one or more facilities. Of course, parents will want to conduct some independent research to determine which of the available facilities has the best reputation. Mothers and fathers should also include their own subjective data in this decision, gleaned from on-site visits and personal interviews with staff members. Not all help is good help, so it is important to be both informed and selective. Financial concerns will also be a factor, though most insurance companies cover fifty to eighty percent of treatment costs, and a number of reputable centers are willing to work out payment plans. It is often less expensive to choose one that operates on a not-for-profit basis and offers a sliding scale for setting fees.

When we suspect our teenagers might be involved in substance abuse, we need to confront them. They may tell us they are only "experimenting" with drugs. They may admit to using marijuana, but deny using anything else. Perhaps they are telling the truth, and perhaps they are telling only a piece of the truth. Let me share a story about a client who was an expert at using partial honesty to deceive his parents.

> When the Johnsons found what looked like drug paraphernalia in their son's room, they immediately confronted him. They had found a large pipe, a couple of small spoons, a few papers, and some white powder. Alarmed, they spoke to their son that evening, expressing their love for him and encouraging him to make a clean breast of any problem he might have so they could be helpful. The son, realizing they were too suspicious to be completely fooled, admitted to smoking marijuana "occasionally," but assured them he had never tried any hard drugs. He was merely holding the spoons and powder for a friend who had brought them over a few days before. The son went on to explain that addictive substances scared him (marijuana should actually be included in that list), and that he had refused to join his friend in

using them. The friend had been pretty cool about it, and they had smoked some pot instead. Unfortunately, the guy had gotten pretty wasted and had forgotten to take the stuff home with him. "Believe me," the fast-talking teen continued, "I would never try anything like that. I shouldn't even have been messing with weed. In fact, I think I might have a problem. It seems like I'm starting to use it more often, even when I don't want to."

Of course, this was extremely upsetting news for the Johnsons, but they were also relieved that their son had trusted them enough to tell the truth. They had friends whose children had been dishonest about drugs, and they were glad that this son was getting it all out in the open. At least now they could find him some help.

They went to a treatment center for some counsel. Because he was only "involved with marijuana," and "willing to get help," an outpatient program was recommended. If he had been known to be using hard drugs, of course, or had he been unwilling to receive assistance, an in-house treatment facility would have been necessary. Incredibly, this young man kept up such a convincing masquerade of recovery that he became addicted to crank and cocaine while attending outpatient treatment for marijuana use!

It is important to realize that people who are using drugs are under the influence of chemicals that render them ready and willing to practice deceit, and sometimes that deceit is cleverly wrapped in selective honesty. If you think this might be the case with your teen, be aware that testing is available. Such testing should be done without warning, because there are many ways to camouflage these drugs in the body, and some drugs stay in the body for such a short duration that a day or two without using will produce a drug-free test result. If the test is not a surprise, it cannot be considered reliable.

If your worst fears are confirmed and you find that your teen is indeed using drugs, it is important to get a thorough assessment immediately. There are good counselors and bad counselors, so do your homework and be a smart consumer. Seek an addiction specialist who works regularly with adolescents and is trained and educated in chemical dependency. The National Council on Alcoholism provides local listings, as do hospitals with chemical dependency units. This person should relate well with your child and be experienced in evaluation, intervention, and treatment. Don't be afraid to ask questions, because your helper's personality style, beliefs, psychological orientation, and level of expertise can make all the difference. A good specialist will advise parents on how to get drug dependent children into treatment as painlessly as possible. Some young people accept help willingly, while others become enraged. For those who resist help, remember that until the age of eighteen parents have every right to place children in treatment, even without consent. It takes a courageous parent to make this step, but love can overcome the fear of a child's hostility. We can keep a teenager's well-being uppermost in our minds, reminding ourselves that he and his feelings are being controlled by chemicals. Once the chemicals leave the body, reason and sanity return. Fences will be mended, resentment turned to gratitude and forgiveness.

As well-meaning parents, we may be reluctant to pursue treatment forcefully, out of concern that we might be infringing upon our children's agency. Agency is not the issue here, because children dependent on drugs are already being deprived of their agency. Helping them reclaim that agency means helping them recover from drug use. The good news is that parents can often influence even the most reluctant children to enter a program voluntarily by exercising appropriate consequences. It would probably be wise to draw up or amend a contract in conjunction with whatever action is taken. If the person in question is eighteen or over, the best chance is to try an intervention, where loved and trusted friends and family members confront the user and try to persuade him to enter a treatment program voluntarily.

Sometimes the mere suggestion of treatment is enough to make a child straighten up for a while, or at least appear to do so. Good advice would be to regard this type of instant cure with suspicion. Delaying intervention because a young person has gotten a job, started going to school again, or is behaving more pleasantly in the home can be a grave mistake. If your child has a problem with drugs, it is unlikely that he or she will be able to sustain these changes without the kind of support that is available in a good treatment program. If treatment is postponed, your teenager's use may spiral into new drugs or increased dosages, all in a desperate attempt to keep up the facade of normalcy. Do not be fooled. It is better to over-treat than under-treat when it comes to substance abuse.

In the event you decide to get your child into a program, your next choice will be whether to select in-house or out-patient therapy. The most important factors to consider—besides your financial circumstances—will be the severity of your child's drug problem, his willingness to accept help, and the status of his emotional health. After consulting your qualified counselor and obtaining his professional opinion, you will want to discuss the overall situation with your parenting partner. Review the information available to you, share your feelings and opinions, make a preliminary determination, and then take it to the Lord. Most of my clients opted for out-patient care, but everyone's needs are different, and this must be settled on a case by case basis. Of course, in cases of deeply ingrained or long-standing drug addiction, a period of inhouse support and detoxification is necessary.

When teens do enter treatment, it will be a family affair. Parents and other siblings are generally expected to participate in therapy, both individual and group. This participation will be important to the user's recovery, as well as to their own. Family members are often devastated by the fallout from a loved one's drug use, and a good therapist can facilitate growth and healing. Fear, anger, loss of trust, codependency, and adaptive family dynamics are only a few of the issues that will need to be discussed. Relationships often have to be rebuilt with new ground rules to support the recovering substance abuser.

Becoming aware of the signs and symptoms of drug use is something all parents of teenagers should do. We need to inform ourselves about substance abuse and discuss it with our children openly, no matter what their ages. Exposing them to community programs and well-researched information will help them make good decisions when the time comes. Sooner than we think, they will have to make choices about whether or not to participate. For some, those choices are already being made. Drug use is more common than most parents imagine, and our children will come face to face with this problem throughout their school years.

The summer before she was to enter high school, a young girl named Amy met some older kids who lived near her beachfront home. They were well-liked, highly esteemed young people who played on the school sports teams and were active in student council, so she was flattered to be included in their activities and hoped they would like her. It didn't take long for this soon-to-be freshman girl to realize that some of the things this group did went against Church standards, and she wasn't exactly sure what to do about it. Many of these teens used bad language, about half of them smoked, and most of them seemed comfortable drinking on the weekends. Their behavior surprised Amy, because in middle school only a few "hard core" groups had been doing things like that. Now, in high school, even the leaders of the school seemed to think that drinking, smoking, and swearing were perfectly okay. Amy knew she didn't want to participate, but she also knew that she would probably want to continue some association with these school leaders, at least on a casual basis. She had always thought of this group as "good" kids and knew that the adults in her community thought so too. In addition, there simply were not many Latter-day Saint kids to hang out with in her stake, and only a handful went to her high school. Amy told herself she would just have to learn how to deal with those friends who, not being Mormon, did not choose Word of Wisdom standards. It would be hard, but Amy felt strong enough to handle it and hoped to be a good example to the kids at her high school.

Summer passed quickly, and the last weekend of vacation arrived. There was going to be a big bonfire on the beach, and Amy looked forward to it. Soon she would be starting high school, and some of the girls had promised to help her make the spirit squad, which she had always wanted to do. When she got to the party, people seemed to be having a great time. Everyone was friendly, and Amy could tell they liked her. All summer long they had been pretty cool about her not drinking or smoking, and no one had pushed her, so she was beginning to relax and feel more comfortable. The evening ended with everyone sitting around the fire. What a fun summer they had shared, and how close they felt as they sat around listening to the waves and watching the flames dance against the darkening sky. Somebody had a guitar, and soon everyone was singing. It was like something out of a movie.

At this point, Amy noticed something being passed around the circle. Looking over, she immediately recognized, because of a drug education class she had taken, a large-bowled pipe called a bong. During that class, she had been selected to role-play how to say no in just this kind of circumstance. Afterwards, she had gone home and talked to her parents about the role-play she had done, and they had discussed the subject further. The next Monday, there had been a special family home evening lesson to follow up. Amy had role-played so many ways to get out of this bad situation that it was almost second nature. Instead of feeling pressured to join in, she reminded herself that if these people were really friends they wouldn't expect her to do anything that went against her beliefs. When the pipe was passed to her, she chose one of the responses her brother had thought of in family home evening and said, "Hey, I'm the Mormon in the group, remember? That makes me the designated driver."

"You can't drive, you're just a baby," teased one

of the older boys. She smiled back at him and replied, "That's right, but I'm in training." Everyone kind of chuckled, the bong went by her, and nothing else was said about it, though she noticed that a couple of other kids let it pass by them too.

Discussing this with her parents later that evening, Amy agreed to avoid unchaperoned activities with these new friends. These parents, though uncomfortable with the situation, felt certain that early training had helped their daughter act wisely under difficult circumstances.

All too often, the environment at school is less than ideal, and our teens need to find ways to deal with the plummeting standards and lowered expectations of today's society. Amy managed to be in the world but not of the world, even in a bad situation, because she was well-prepared. She knew in advance how to respond. Unfortunately, too many of our young people do not have such favorable outcomes. Even Amy might have reacted differently during a period of acute stress or sadness. Good training in the home is not magic, and a lot depends upon the child's state of mind at the time temptation comes knocking.

We need to be aware of how our teenagers are feeling about themselves. Effective parenting can build and boost a child's self-esteem. If we make it our business to educate ourselves in this regard, beginning with the methods and information set out in Chapters 4 and 5 and including ideas gleaned from other sources, we can and will make a difference for our children. Even a teen who is doing well may become vulnerable if something changes in his life. A move, the loss of a friend, a difficult year at school, physical changes, family conflicts, illness, and other deceptively commonplace problems can render a previously well-insulated child vulnerable to drugs. We should keep our eyes open and our spirits in tune and not be afraid to act, if necessary, in behalf of our young people. They may not appreciate it at the moment, but they will thank us for it later.

It's wise to remember that no one is immune and that good kids from good families can have problems with drugs. As Latter-day Saints, we have the opportunity to unite with other parents and increase drug awareness in ourselves, our youth, and our youth programs. Prevention requires attention. Pulling the wool over our eyes, however tempting, is like conceding the battle to the adversary. Instead, we can encourage youth who are drug-free to stay drug-free. We can love and support teens who have fallen prey to drugs by suspending judgment and offering needed assistance to them and their families. We can provide the necessary structure, as a community, for families who are struggling with the effects of drug abuse. This is a battle we cannot afford to concede, because this is a battle that can be won.

A Word about Depression

Even in a troubled world, parents are often shocked to learn of the rising tide of teenage depression. We look back with nostalgia on the carefree days when teenagers and depression seemed an unlikely match. Today, teenagers are experiencing bouts of depression in increasing numbers. Stress at school, emphasis on material things, indulgence in worldly pursuits, pressure about looks and weight, crime, domestic violence, broken or dysfunctional families, childhood traumas, drug use, and more assault the emotional health and well-being of our children. This reality explains why parents need to be aware of the signs and symptoms of depression. The American Psychiatric Association lists the major criteria for diagnosing depression as follows:

"1. depressed mood (or it can be an irritable mood in adolescents)
2. apathy, loss of interest or pleasure in usual activities
3. significant weight loss or gain (change in eating habits)
4. restlessness or sluggishness
5. sleeping too much or too little
6. fatigue
7. feelings of worthlessness or guilt
8. inability to think clearly or concentrate, or make decisions
9. thoughts of death or suicide

At least five of these symptoms must be present during the same two-week period for a diagnosis of depression to be made" (*Diagnostic and Statistical Manual of Mental Disorders*, 3rd edition, revised. Washington, D.C.: American Psychiatric Association [1987], 222).

When teenagers suffer from depression that lasts more than two weeks, they need professional assistance. As parents, we cannot be helpful unless we are aware of the problem. We often attribute symptoms to the usual teenage ups and downs or changing hormones, and sometimes we are right. However, just as with drug abuse, it is safer to err on the side of caution and have a child evaluated by a professional if his or her behavior changes for a period of time.

Parents can be supportive and watchful of a teen who is having emotional difficulties. If depression is the problem, therapy will probably be recommended. In the case of a chemical imbalance, medication may even be advised. Sometimes a teenager will try to self-medicate with drugs and alcohol. Needless to say, illegal substances and depression can be a deadly combination. Additionally, people suffering from mood disorders may experience more distress as they undergo treatment for substance abuse, particularly if they have not been treated for the underlying condition.

A teenager who speaks of ending his life should be taken seriously. Young people are impulsive, and thinking about suicide is a red flag that should not be ignored. Too many parents have lived to regret their assumption that a child was just in a black mood or only trying to get attention. In fact, any teen who uses conversation about suicide to get attention should be given attention, immediately. Writing about suicide is also cause for concern.

There is a lot of good help for troubled teens, but we need to be selective in finding a therapist our teenager likes and respects. After making certain all candidates are qualified, effective with adolescents, and willing and able to work within a Latter-day Saint paradigm, we should choose the one our child prefers, instead of making the mistake of choosing the therapist we like best. When a child is not connecting with the counselor, we are wasting our time and money. Even worse, we are forfeiting the chance to get the help we seek. A good rule of thumb is that if a solid connection has not been established within six weeks, it is time to move on. The bottom line is this: If the teenager isn't talking, nothing is going to happen.

The purpose of this chapter is not to frighten, but to inform. Forewarned is forearmed, and the actions we take with our teens in crisis can make all the difference in their physical, emotional, and spiritual well-being. In other words, knowing really is half the battle, because it gives us the power to act. Teenagers today are beset by circumstances and temptations most parents could never have imagined. They need more than love and support. They need parents who know what their children are up against, parents who are willing and able to throw them that life preserver when the waters get too rough.

HELPS AND HINTS

WARNING SIGNS OF DRUG INVOLVEMENT

Is your child losing interest in or being dropped from extracurricular activities?

Has your child stopped turning in assignments, or does he fail to complete them?

Have your child's grades fallen?

Is he being difficult in class?

Has he started cutting school, or is he habitually truant?

Is he losing respect for rules and authority figures?

Has he been suspended from school, or expelled?

Is he sleeping more?

Has he changed friends?

Do his new friends have a different look than the old ones?

Do the new friends avoid you, or does your child avoid
    being at home?
Does he use slang associated with drugs?
Is he dressing differently; liking different music?
Does he argue with the family?
Does he do his jobs around the house?
Is he respecting curfew?
Is he obeying the rules of the family?
Does he still like to participate in activities with parents
    and siblings?
Does he stay out overnight or leave the house without
    asking?
Is he alone in his room a lot?
Does he enjoy family vacations and family visits?
Does he seem to be hiding things from you?
Does he willingly tell you where he's going or who he'll
    be with?
Does he get angry easily? Do you have to be careful what
    you say?
Does he have money you can't account for?
Has his language deteriorated? Is he swearing or shouting
    at family members?
Is he quiet and withdrawn, unwilling to talk?
Is he becoming hostile?
Has he ever hit or pushed family members?
Has he destroyed family property?
Does he keep his word?
Does he seem to have trouble paying attention to things?
Does he criticize activities or friends he used to enjoy?
Is he restless?
Has he gained or lost weight?
Does he get sick more often?
Are his sleeping habits unusual?

Has his room or appearance gone downhill?
Does he change his clothes regularly?
Does he seem to have too much or too little energy?
Is he eating more than he used to?
Is he moody? Do his moods swing?
Will he discuss his behavior or does he get defensive?
Is he losing interest in things he once liked?
Is he motivated?
Has he been selling his belongings, or other people's?
Is he doing things he didn't used to believe in?
Does he tell the truth?
Has he been caught cheating on tests, lying?
Does he attend church? Believe in God?
Has he dropped or does he ridicule friends he used to have
　　at church?

Please note that this list is not all-inclusive, and your child may not demonstrate all symptoms or may show other signs not listed.

Helpful Phone Numbers

Just Say No International (800) 258–2766
National Institute on Drug Abuse (800) 662-HELP (4357)

Reflections

Imagine an evening sky,
the moon and stars
its only source of illumination.
Now add to that scenario
a dazzling display of fireworks.
How easily the pure light
of the moon and stars
is eclipsed
by the sparkling colors,
yet how quickly those glittering sparks of color
fade away into nothingness.
The adversary
lures our teens
with his beguiling fireworks.
He entices them away
from the true light and leaves them
with nothing but darkness and shadows.
This has always been his method,
but the advent of the Second Coming
has made him even more bold.
Today,
we are witnessing a spectacle—
the grand finale of his fireworks show,
a display the likes of which
the world has never seen.
No wonder
so many of our youth
are trading the moon and stars
for manufactured light
and coming up empty.

CHAPTER

10

TAKING YOURSELF
OUT OF THE DRIVER'S SEAT

WE ARE ALL on a difficult journey, but the road seems
longer and the hills steeper when we travel in fear of losing a child. The pioneers said good-bye to many children
along the way, but even their sad losses were not eternal
ones. There is nothing more painful than seeing children
we have loved and taught go astray, casting aside eternal
goals. It is easy to become discouraged when we realize
they sit in the driver's seat, and we do not. Sometimes
there is a temptation to figuratively jump into the car,
wrestle the wheel from their hands, and take control. That
kind of action would be appropriate if a child needed hos-
pitalization for chemical dependency or severe emotional
illness, but even then, control would need to be surren-
dered as soon as the teen became capable of making ratio-
nal decisions and using agency.

There is wisdom in the gentle prodding of President
Ezra Taft Benson: "Our pattern, or model, for [parent]hood

is our Heavenly Father. How does He work with His children?" (*The Teachings of Ezra Taft Benson* [1988], 503). Elder Marion D. Hanks answers this question with the following example: "Consider another family in which one choice son humbly accepted the counsel and plan of his father and followed that plan according to this father's will, while another son, also an authority in the kingdom of his father, followed his own wayward will and base arrogance, rebelled against his father and his instructions, and, not content with this, induced a third of his brothers and sisters to rebel against their father and to follow him, to their own heartbreak and sorrow." Elder Hanks goes on to say, "To those to whom the sorrow of a child unresponsive to parental instruction and example has come, be comforted. God understands. He knows what it means to have a rebellious son and wayward children" (in Conference Report, April 1967, 126).

Let us return once more to the words of Joseph F. Smith, who said, "However wayward they might be, . . . when you speak or talk to them, do it not in anger, do it not harshly, in a condemning spirit. . . . Use no lash and no violence, but . . . reason—approach them with reason, with persuasion and love unfeigned." Acting out of anger is not an option when we are parenting by Heavenly Father's example. President Smith continued: "You can coax them; you can lead them, . . . but you can't drive them; they won't be driven. We won't be driven. Men are not in the habit of being driven; they are not made that way.

"This is not the way that God intended, in the beginning, to deal with his children—by force. . . .

"You can't force your boys, nor your girls into heaven. You may force them to hell, by using harsh means in the efforts to make them good, when you yourselves are not as good as you should be" (*Gospel Doctrine*, 316–17). Apparently, interfering with agency is not an option either.

Brother Gallagher was a man who lived and died by principle. He and his pioneer forebears had held to the rod for many generations, and there was a proud family tradition of honor and righteous living. The man loved and was proud of his family. He did have high expectations, but asked nothing of his children that had not been asked of him. These were difficult times to bring up a child, but Brother Gallagher would not allow his family to be touched by the evils of the world. He taught correct principles as he had been taught, and he and his would live by those principles.

The Gallaghers were a good family, and most of their six children accepted and valued the beliefs their father espoused. One son, however, seemed to question his authority. This child had always been a little hard to handle, but over the years his father had managed to control the boy's behavior by tightening the reins a little. The last year of junior high, this became more difficult. The son started growing his hair long and began bringing over friends that made Brother Gallagher uneasy. When his grades dropped the following semester, the irate father decided it was time to put his foot down. He forbade his son to see the friends in question and ordered him to get a haircut. Willfully, the son refused to obey, openly defying his father for the first time. Shocked, Brother Gallagher repeated his instructions, only to have the young man answer with an obscenity. Desperate to regain control, Brother Gallagher struck his child several times, forcibly escorting him to a friend's home to have his hair cut. He then told the unhappy teenager that he would be under house arrest until he agreed to cut off the relationships with his undesirable friends. Furthermore, he would not be talking on the phone, watching TV, or listening to the radio until he had at least four A's on his report card.

On the surface, improvements were made. The hair was short. Though the face was sulky, the grades went up, and the unsavory friends were nowhere to be seen. Within a couple of months, the house arrest was lifted. To all appearances, things seemed to be under control. Brother Gallagher felt relieved and pleased that he had found the fortitude to enforce stern but necessary measures. Spare the rod and spoil the child was as true today as it ever had been. He was glad he loved his son enough to keep him on the straight and narrow.

Meanwhile, this completely stifled son was angry, very angry. The rebellious teen told his forbidden friends that his father had beaten him, and he continued to meet with those friends secretly, during hours he was supposed to be working part-time in a nearby factory. He acted out his rebellion in private, using chewing tobacco and drinking. Of course, he kept his hair short and hid his real feelings, but the anger continued to grow and fester inside him. Occasionally, he would explode. Then he and his father would have vicious shouting matches, after which he would be hit or grounded. To avoid this, he would try harder to keep his anger hidden, but hiding it only seemed to make things worse. Who was his father to make all his decisions for him? If the old man was so religious, what made him think he could beat his son just for telling him what he really thought? What kind of church was it that didn't let a person have any ideas of his own?

Things really came to a head when Brother Gallagher learned from a ward member that his son had been smoking in the school parking lot, with the very group of friends he had supposedly stopped seeing. Feeling betrayed, the father flew into a rage, which escalated when he confronted his son and was finally allowed a glimpse of how unrepentant the young man actually was. Infuriated by his son's lack of respect for the family and sincerely afraid for the boy's spiritual survival, Brother Gallagher could think of no other way to help his son than by trying to control his behavior completely. The distraught father spent the next couple of years inflicting physical punishment and imposing house arrest. In fact, as a junior, the young man was under house arrest for an entire year, leaving the house only to go to church and school. During that time, this completely alienated son made it clear to everyone, even ward members, that he hated his father and would leave home the minute he was old enough.

The day he turned eighteen, Brother Gallagher's son was gone. That was well over three years ago, and they haven't spoken since. Friends of the family are aware that the troubled young man is living an unrighteous and unhealthy lifestyle. It seems that Brother Gallagher's best efforts to force his child to heaven, however well-meant, not only fell short, but failed entirely.

In deference to President Smith's counsel not to drive our children, how can we take ourselves out of those drivers' seats and be "as good as we should be" in helping our teenagers find their way? To take the car analogy a little further, if grabbing the wheel is inappropriate, what are some alternatives? Perhaps our young people might allow us to sit down beside them, particularly when our behavior has won enough trust to merit a place in their vehicles. If our behavior has not earned that level of trust, we will want to make necessary adjustments and begin to earn it. Elder Ezra Taft Benson counseled: "Live close to your children, that you have their love and confidence, that you are not harsh, that you are not cross, that you are understanding. Be firm in the right—yes, in a kindly, sweet way. I pray that the time will never come when your children will go to others for counsel and advice which you should be giving them" ("I'll Go Where You Want Me to Go," *Church News*, 23 Nov. 1946, 8). They will always do better with a caring parent in the passenger seat, helping them navigate.

Of course, there are times when we have done all we can and our teenagers still refuse to let us in the car. Maybe we have been kindly, sweet, and laudably "firm in the right," but it seems to have made no difference. Our children may love us with all their hearts yet continue to make it very clear that they simply do not want us sitting next to them. It does happen. In cases like these, we can still put up road signs to guide them and street lights to help them see clearly. We can even remind them that they have their own headlights, if they will just remember to use them.

It is, after all, our responsibility to bring up our children in light and truth (see D&C 93:40), and we must do all we can to follow that admonition. We must also respect agency and realize that there will be, as Elder Hanks warns, "good parents who strive earnestly to bring up their children in the way they should go, only to have those children use their individuality and agency to follow other ways." To these, Elder Hanks says, "The Lord has forcefully taught us that in his eyes 'the son shall not bear the iniquity of the father, neither shall the father bear the iniquity of the son' (Ezekiel 18:20). Each accountable person must ultimately answer for his own decisions" (in Conference Report, April 1970, 132). In other words, there will be those parents who do all that they can do, who try their very best, only to have their children disregard their teachings and choose their own way. To them, Elder Joseph Fielding Smith said, "If parents have done all in their power to teach their children correctly by example and precept and the children then go astray, the parents will not be held responsible and the sin will be upon the children" (Doctrines of Salvation, comp. Bruce R. McConkie [1954], 1:316).

This is small comfort to grieving parents whose immediate fears are centered not on their own eternal salvation, but on the eternal salvation of their wayward children. Where can these parents find solace? A good beginning might be in trusting God, who was and is the first parent of every child ever born into this world. We can place our trust in God the Father, having faith that He knows what our children need and will do the best He can for them. We can remind ourselves that Heavenly Father's best is pretty good—no, more than good—perfect! We can also trust in our children, remembering that they exist as our spirit equals, strong beings who chose to come to earth and work out their eternal salvation before the Lord. President Ezra Taft Benson reminded us that "as we look into their faces and contemplate their needs, we might well consider that some of them were probably choicer spirits up there than we were" (God, Family, Country: Our Three Great Loyalties [1974], 172). Maybe we can exercise some faith in their ability, given all we and Father in Heaven can do to help, to choose wisely—to find their way back to the straight and narrow path we are pointing out so desperately.

What else can we do? We can make a plan and stay with it, just as our Father in Heaven made a plan and has stayed with it. There is balance and stability and justice in the execution of a righteous plan. Let us follow the example given us. Our job is to establish a plan, and our children's job is to make the choices they came here to make. Heavenly Father will help both of us fulfill our assignments, if we are willing to ask Him.

This brings us to prayer, a powerful tool we can use in helping our children. We need to be sure we are praying with the right purpose, or our prayers may not be answered. What will Father's answer be if our prayers are just another attempt to control? "Make my child do this. . . . Make my child see that." Surely our prayers are much more effective when we pray that our children will be blessed with the opportunities and experiences they need to remember who they are and why they came to earth. We can ask that they be blessed with strength, wisdom, and the ability to see clearly. We can petition that we, as parents, will know what the Lord would have us do. We can pray for the will to do those things.

We may accomplish all of this and still find ourselves wishing we could do more. At this point we can recommit to doing the same things a little bit better, or maybe a whole lot better. Sadly, even this might not be enough. In spite of every valiant effort, our children may choose not to respond, to continue on a course that pains us and endangers them. As agonizing as this can be, we will need to keep ourselves out of the driver's seat and remember that we can only do what we can do. Heavenly Father's example is ours to follow. He has always known His part;

the rest is up to each individual spirit. "Every man must stand before God and answer for his own choices and for his own character" (Marion D. Hanks, in Conference Report, April 1967, 125).

Because this is a particularly sobering thought for parents, let me close with some words of hope from President Spencer W. Kimball:

"I have sometimes seen children of good families rebel, resist, stray, sin, and even actually fight God. In this they bring sorrow to their parents, who have done their best to set in movement a current and to teach and live as examples. But I have repeatedly seen many of these same children, after years of wandering, mellow, realize what they have been missing, repent, and make great contribution to the spiritual life of their community. The reason I believe this can take place is that, despite all the adverse winds to which these people have been subjected, they have been influenced still more, and much more than they realized, by the current of life in the homes in which they were reared. When, in later years, they feel a longing to recreate in their own families the same atmosphere they enjoyed as children, they are likely to turn to the faith that gave meaning to their parents' lives.

"There is no guarantee, of course, that righteous parents will succeed always in holding their children, and certainly they may lose them if they do not do all in their power. The children have their free agency.

"What we do know is that righteous parents who strive to develop wholesome influences for their children will be held blameless at the last day, and that they will succeed in saving most of their children, if not all" ("Ocean Currents and Family Influences," *Ensign*, Nov. 1974, 110).

His is truly a message of comfort and inspiration for all of us.

HELPS AND HINTS

A Parent's Reverie

"Who shall ascend into the hill of the Lord? or who shall stand in his holy place?" (Psalm 24:3).

> Sometimes when I am quite alone, and still,
> The Spirit speaks, and whispers words of truth:
> That I am not the master of your youth,
> And was not called to bend you to my will.
>
> I was not called to bend you to my will,
> Nor would He have me bind you to His own.
> His yoke is one that you must bear alone;
> I cannot thirst for you, nor drink your fill.
>
> I cannot thirst for you, nor drink your fill,
> Though living water springs forth pure and sweet;
> Yet I can but direct your wand'ring feet,
> For you must tread the path and climb the hill.
>
> For you must tread the path and climb the hill
> That leads you back into His warm embrace.
> I see you standing in His holy place,
> Sometimes when I am quite alone, and still.

EPILOGUE

THE CIVIL RIGHTS movement has gone a long way on three words: "Keep hope alive." I like these words because hope is indeed a living thing, much like the love we bear for our children. In my life, this book has been a living thing as well, and I have, in a sense, given birth to it, but hope is the spark that inspired its creation. When President David O. McKay said, "The sun of hope is rising" (*Gospel Ideals* [1953], 387), he was speaking to our generation as clearly as if he were here on earth today. His words are for every one of us, who as Latter-day Saints "believe all things, . . . hope all things, . . . have endured many things, and hope to be able to endure all things" (Articles of Faith 1:13). Hope is our birthright, for we are sons and daughters of a Heavenly Father who loves us dearly, a Father who will do all within His power to welcome us home.

His message to parents is simple: Have faith. Believe with "a perfect brightness of hope" (2 Nephi 31:20). Refuse to give up on the young people you love. Refuse to give up on each other. The apostle Paul promises that "in due season we shall reap, if we faint not" (Galatians 6:9). As parents in Zion, may the Lord magnify us to that end.

INDEX

Abuse, substance, 11, 22, 66, 76, 95–99; loss of child to, 113; prevention of, 122–23; treatment of, and mood disorders, 125; physical, 133–34

Accountability, 33, 55, 82; and responsibility, 47

Activities, extracurricular, a mother's, 35

Addiction, 11, 76, 94–95; specialist in treating, 117

Adolescence, 6

Affection, and boundaries, 35

Agency, 74, 93–94, 99–100; abuse of, 24; free, 42–44, 139; and drug use, 117–18

Alcohol, 11

American Psychiatric Association, 124

Anger, 18, 54–55, 93, 134; and communication, 104

"A Parent's Reverie," 140

Approval, 92

"A Promise for Eternity," 29–30

Arrest, house, of child, 134–35

Authority, 41, 47; reestablishing, 77

Behavior: changes in, 14; self-destructive, 41, 44–45

Belief: in self, 56; in children, 141

Benson, Ezra Taft, 131–32, 136, 137

Betrayal, sense of, 103, 135

Blackmail, emotional, 55, 90

Blame, 21, 25, 63

Blessing: patriarchal, 56; priesthood, 97–98

Boundaries, setting, 35

Chastity, 114

Children, control of, 23–24

Choice, 36, 42–43

Church of Jesus Christ of Latter-day Saints, The: representing, 51; standards of, 120; rebellion against, 110, 134

Comfort, 105

Communication and anger, 104

Community, developing sense of, 53–54

Compromise, 64–65

Conflict, handling, 65, 81–82

Consequences, 33, 47; logical, 56–57; enforceable, 66, 103; limits and, 76; of smoking, 95–96; and contracts, 105

Consistency, 109

Contracts, 57, 70–72; negotiating, 73; and consequences, 105

Control, 131, 133–35; limits of,